Puttin' on the

Grits™

Puttin' on the

A GUIDE TO SOUTHERN ENTERTAINING

Grits™

Deborah Ford

Illustrated by
Mary Lynn Blasutta

A PLUME BOOK

PLUME
Published by Penguin Group
Penguin Group (USA) Inc., 375 Hudson Street, New York, New York 10014, U.S.A.
Penguin Group (Canada), 90 Eglinton Avenue East, Suite 700, Toronto, Ontario,
Canada M4P 2Y3 (a division of Pearson Penguin Canada Inc.)
Penguin Books Ltd., 80 Strand, London WC2R 0RL, England
Penguin Ireland, 25 St. Stephen's Green, Dublin 2, Ireland (a division of Penguin Books Ltd.)
Penguin Group (Australia), 250 Camberwell Road, Camberwell, Victoria 3124, Australia
(a division of Pearson Australia Group Pty. Ltd.)
Penguin Books India Pvt. Ltd., 11 Community Centre, Panchsheel Park,
New Delhi – 110 017, India
Penguin Books (NZ), cnr Airborne and Rosedale Roads, Albany, Auckland 1310,
New Zealand (a division of Pearson New Zealand Ltd.)
Penguin Books (South Africa) (Pty.) Ltd., 24 Sturdee Avenue, Rosebank,
Johannesburg 2196, South Africa

Penguin Books Ltd., Registered Offices: 80 Strand, London WC2R 0RL, England

Published by Plume, a member of Penguin Group (USA) Inc. Previously published in a
Dutton edition.

First Plume Printing, January 2006
10   9   8   7   6   5   4   3   2   1

Ⓟ   REGISTERED TRADEMARK—MARCA REGISTRADA

The Library of Congress has catalogued the Dutton edition as follows:
Ford, Deborah.
    Puttin on the grits : a guide to southern entertaining / Deborah Ford.
        p.   cm.
    ISBN 0-525-94868-6 (hc.)
    ISBN 0-452-28689-1 (pbk.)
1. Entertaining. I. Title.
    TX731 F66 2005
    642'.4—dc22   2005041270

Printed in the United States of America
Original hardcover design by Sabrina Bowers
Illustrated by Mary Lynn Blasutta

This book is dedicated to my beautiful daughters,
Callie and Chesley Michael.
You have been the loves of my life and a blessing.

People who don't believe in miracles
haven't met my newfound angels,
Becky Crossfield and Terrie Puma.

Contents

Acknowledgments

I would like to express my most sincere appreciation to my business partner, Don Sallee, for his continued support. Special thanks to Elizabeth Butler-Witter for the countless hours you have spent on this book. Your hard work, creativity, and writing have helped make this book possible. Many thanks to my editor, Trena Keating, as well as Emily Haynes, Peter McGuigan, and Bret Witter. Thanks to Wendy Tunstill and Dana Gache for your ongoing hard work, dedication, and friendship during all of my Grits projects. And of course, I want to express my thanks to all of my wonderful Southern Sisters.

Introduction

As I traveled the South during my book tour for *The GRITS Guide to Life*, I had the pleasure of visiting places all over this beautiful region—from the smallest bookstores to the largest regional television stations. No matter where I visited, I was welcomed with open arms and smiling faces. Southerners want to make their guests comfortable and happy.

I have spoken to women at country clubs, libraries, and department stores, and everywhere I go, I hear the same story: Our Southern way of life is diminishing too quickly. Southern ladies and gentlemen are afraid that their children and grandchildren will not know, and will be unable to pass on, all the wonderful things that have been in their families for generations. The secret of the perfect biscuit, bringing out the best tablecloth for Sunday supper as a family, jarring pickled peaches at the height of summer: All are being lost to a world of fast food and traffic jams.

Unfortunately, I am guilty, too. Guilty of not spending more time with my own daughters, Callie and Chesley, and not teaching them all the things they should know about their roots. When I pass on, who is going to make Grandma Emma's perfect dumplings? As a single mother, I felt I had a pretty good excuse for not taking that extra time. After touring the South—boy, do I feel guilty! Entertaining in the

South is about friends and family, and if people like me don't make the time to share our traditions, who will?

Whether I was visiting a country club or a discount store, the pride that I saw in the faces was the same. Whether we drink from Waterford crystal or mason jars, whether we own a mansion or polish the floors, we share a common Southern identity. We value tradition, we value manners, and we value our families. The look in our eyes when we remember the tastes and smells of home is the same, and we have the same need to preserve what is good about our Southern heritage.

My children had a lot more worldly wealth than I did coming up, but they missed out on a lot of other important things. My best memories growing up in north Alabama are the simple gatherings with our neighbors. Mr. Oakley would make ice cream and sing for hours. While he was singing on the front porch (wasn't the world nicer when all houses had porches out front?), the neighborhood children would catch fireflies. He was a man who knew how to entertain, though I doubt he could fold a napkin if his life depended on it. His warm spirit was entertainment enough. After church on Sunday, everybody would gather at Ms. Mattie's house. She made the best food I've had, before or since (though all those hugs and kisses she gave were part of the special seasoning). Ms. Mattie was a real lady, even if she never had much, and I'd be as proud to be a guest at her house in the country as I would be to dine at the White House.

Our neighbors (and back then, our neighbors and our families were often one and the same) were together for all life's celebrations: the weddings, graduations, birthdays, baby showers, and funerals. Entertaining wasn't about trying to outdo the neighbors. It wasn't about lobster and tarte tatin for twenty. (I'd rather have Ms. Mattie's fried chicken and cream gravy any day.) It was about being together, enjoying life's milestones, helping one another in times of need. We celebrated—and cried—together. I've had no better food, comfort, or joy in my life than I had at the celebrations in that small town.

That's what this book is about—entertaining the Southern way. Entertaining in the South is about making everyone feel welcome and want to be around you, whether you're a host or a guest. And entertaining Southern style is about family, good friends, and making the most out of life, no matter how humble it may be. It's about preserving our proud traditions and the simple life of our ancestors before the crazy modern world takes over.

This world is changing, and we Pearl Girls are changing with it, but what makes us so special, what gives us our charm, is that we can change while knowing how to leave well enough alone. That's the Southern way, and the Pearl Girl way, and I hope these pages share a little bit of that special Southern charm with you.

Mr. Oakley's Southern-Style Party

1 front porch and swing
1 jigger of fireflies
1 ice cream churn
1 heaping handful of friends and family
pinch of love

Stir all ingredients together. Season to taste with old-fashioned singing. Makes enough to serve the neighborhood, with plenty left to share.

CHAPTER 1

Southern Entertaining— More Than a Hootenanny

> With the South itself, no other form of cultural expression, not even music, is as distinctly characteristic of the region as the spreading of a feast of native food and drink before a gathering of kin and friends.
>
> —JOHN EGERTON
> SOUTHERN FOOD, AT HOME,
> ON THE ROAD, IN HISTORY

> When it comes right down to it, Southern hospitality is born of a unique lifestyle; one of grace and style faced with a deep appreciation for leisure and laughter . . . it is a blend of many honorable virtues passed down through generations—gentleness, kindness, and the receiving of strangers and friends alike with openness, selflessness, and caring.
>
> —EMYL JENKINS
> EMYL JENKINS' SOUTHERN HOSPITALITY

S TART POLISHING THE SILVER, LIGHT THE CANDLES, AND ice down sweet tea or—goodness, honey—just pull out some paper plates and pop open a six pack. . . . We're having a party, Southern style! A Southern girl knows how to entertain, whether it's throwing an intimate dinner party for eight or a catered affair for eight hundred. Maybe she's putting the finishing touches on a handmade wedding cake, or maybe she's putting the store-bought sweets on her mama's china. Either way, she does it with a smile on her face that makes every guest feel welcomed.

Southern parties and Southern hostesses are different from those in the rest of the country. Entertaining is more gentle, more traditional, and centers more around the home. You're likely to sip a drink on someone's porch before you meet up at a bar. We value Mama's china (and her gracious good manners), but we also know we can use it to serve arroz con pollo or sushi. Southern parties, and Southern women, are the very best of the old and the new.

In my mind, there are five elements that make Southern parties what they are:

1. *the front porch* (friends and neighbors)
2. *sweet tea* (tradition)
3. *Grandma's silver* (family)

4. *Christmas oranges* (going out of our way)
5. *champagne* (bringing in a new sparkle)

So let's walk through them.

The Front Porch
(Friends and Neighbors)

Southern entertaining begins on the front porch. Once, the front porch was the gathering place for people to talk. Some folks—men, mostly—call it gossip. The porch is where people would gather, sit in the shade, drink sweet tea, and wait for someone to walk by to join them and share the "news." Back then, the news wasn't about shootings or terrorism but about what was happening in the lives of the people we knew and loved, or at least tolerated. The front porch was where we gathered on our porch swings and rocking chairs and gently rocked to the slower rhythm of Southern life. We Southerners still have a "front porch" philosophy of life—a bit more relaxed, a bit more sharing, and a bit more welcoming than is found in other parts of the world.

SOUTHERN TRANSLATION

hootenanny [hōōt´ ə na nē] n. *an old-fashioned gathering to hear and share good old Kentucky bluegrass music; a foot-stompin' good time; what happens whenever two Pearl Girls get together. (Get out of the way, boys!)*

Southern entertaining is the same as it always has been at its heart. No matter whether it's a wedding, a baby shower, a cocktail party, a cookout, a bar mitzvah, a hunt breakfast, Christmas, or Kwanzaa, a Southern party is about the front porch of the heart. It's about gathering together to share the news, whether life carries us to a South Carolina feed and seed or a New York penthouse. It's about being together to share ourselves and our love. And whether we can afford plywood or teak, it's about setting a spell and rocking to the rhythms of Southern life. And, honey, most of all, it's about having a good old time.

Sweet Tea (Tradition)

There was a time when if you sat down to a meal in the South, from the humblest farm to the fanciest white tablecloth restaurant, you'd be offered tea. And that meant one thing—old-fashioned, homemade sweet tea. Not unsweetened, not hot, and not (heaven forbid) powdered, but that rich, orange concoction that refreshed even on the most dusty August day. Sweet tea was the Southern beverage of choice, welcomed by hard-partying honky-tonk men and Baptist preachers alike. Sweet tea to us Southerners was what wine is to the French. Without it, Grandma's biscuits or Aunt Sissy's chicken-fried steak just wouldn't be the same. It was a tradition that brought us together and always meant a taste of home.

Sweet tea wasn't something that you whipped up in an instant. If you took shortcuts, you'd end up with something cloudy and bitter. Southern sweet tea was like Southern life—it was all the richer and sweeter because we took the

The Power Lunch—
Southern Style

Up North, a power lunch means sitting in a chichi restaurant and planning to take over the world. Down South, things are a bit different. The office where I work has a break room outfitted with everything from a double sink to a gas range. Five or six of us decided that we were sick of brown-bagging tuna and leftovers, and we decided to take turns cooking for the group. We'd all make a meal the night before and leave it warming in the oven until lunchtime.

For weeks, the aromas of casseroles, soups, chilies, roasts, stews, cobblers, and—oh, honey—goodness knows what else, seeped out of the break room, infiltrating every office and sometimes even the plant next door. Mouths watered and appetites grew. Coworkers stared sadly at leftover pork chops nuked in the microwave or a peanut butter and jelly sandwich squashed under notes from the morning meeting while the smell of Julie's glazed ham and homemade corn bread or Barbara's green bean casserole drifted their way. Soon, there were about a dozen of us, and our get-together was looking a lot more like Sunday dinner with the whole family than like a group of coworkers slamming down a quick lunch. We used our entire lunch hour, and sometimes a bit more when hot banana bread and butter or a refreshing fruit salad beckoned.

Some of us were no doubt putting more time and effort into lunch than for supper with the spouse and children, but with so many of us, we had to cook only once or twice a month. The rest of the time, all we had to do was sit back and indulge. We started showcasing family recipes that had been handed down from our mamas and grannies. Questions like, "The baked beans are delicious—what did you put in them?" were answered with, "Oh, that's my aunt Rose's recipe. She got it from her mother-in-law. Ain't it good?" Why, we had some of the best sharing ever—a lot better than you'd hear at a real power lunch.

As good as that food and conversation were, though, once Joe joined up, we were all outdone. Joe worked out in the plant and was drawn in by his nose. He was always laughing—an ordained minister with a permanent smile—and you could tell from his belly that his parishioners had been doing a fine job feeding him! He was Cajun born and raised in "Nawlins," and his jambalaya was rich and spicy but still smooth and easy. You've never tasted such a meal. Something special and mysterious—maybe a touch of voodoo—made that food dance on our plates and in our mouths. The seafood gumbo, steamy as a summer night on the bayou, had a spell all its own. We ate like folks possessed and were filled to the gills when Joe brought out the crowning glory—warm, homemade sweet potato pies. "Too full," we protested (a bit halfheartedly, I admit, once I saw that sweet orange goodness).

Joe laughed from his belly on down to his toes. "Gots to have dessawt!" he said. And, I declare, we all did.

—Charlyne Morrison
Cartersville, Georgia

time to do it right. You had to bring a half gallon of water to a boil and steep two family-sized bags of tea for no more than four minutes, stir in as much sugar as you and your diabetes can take, and let it set until cool. Then you added water to taste and chilled it just right. If you followed your mother's recipe and did it just so, you'd have the perfect glass of home. Southern parties still have sweet tea at their heart. They're a reflection of our traditions and of ourselves, a taste that brings us back to what we once were and what we can try to be.

A PEARL GIRL KNOWS

Stirring a packet of sugar into a glass of cold tea won't give you real Southern iced tea flavor. Always add your sweetener when the tea is still as warm as the heart of a Southern belle.

When I was a little girl, life in the South was much simpler. My parents were sharecroppers, and we lived in the little town of Tanner, Alabama. People then didn't just pack up and move to California or Alaska or Timbuktu. We lived on the same land where our parents and grandparents had farmed, and when it came time to settle down, we'd build a little house right near to our people.

SOUTHERN TRANSLATION

rippit [rip´ it] n. *a wild, noisy party.*
ex: "When we girls get together, we rip it up and have a rippit."

*Five Ways to Bring the Front Porch
Back into Your Life (Whether You Live in a
High-Rise Condo or a Plantation Manor)*

1. Make up a batch of your favorite cookies, write down the recipe by hand (and, better yet, the story of where you got the recipe), and deliver them to a neighbor you don't know very well.

2. Buy two-serving bags of coffee, hand them out to friends you haven't spoken to for a while with notes reading, "Let's get together to share this sometime."

3. Schedule a "date" with one of your children (or your significant other). Order a pizza, turn off the phone (and cell phone and BlackBerry—anything that beeps), and spend a couple of hours together.

4. Visit a nursing home, and talk to the residents. Bring a handful of magazines and paperbacks for entertainment. Remember, the front porch can be anywhere people need to talk!

5. Host a trivia night for the neighborhood. Place an invitation in each mailbox with a couple of facts about yourself and your family, and say that you just want to get to know the neighbors better. Have questions about your state and city or town. (This is especially good if you're a Southern native and you live near newcomers.) You'd be surprised how fast your living room becomes the front porch for the whole neighborhood!

Things have changed a lot since then, and in a lot of ways for the better. I'd much rather be writing these books than working from before dawn and worrying about the rain, the drought, and the pests. (Besides, working the land would mess up my beautiful manicure—my hands might have calluses from my younger days, but I'm proud of them.) Life is a lot easier. But in a lot of ways, it's harder, too. Since we move around a lot more, holding on to tradition has become a bigger challenge.

Goodness Gracious!

Kudzu was introduced to the South during the dust bowl of the 1930s. Like a lot of transplants to the South, kudzu turned out to love its new home (maybe a bit too much). We've all seen trees, electric poles, and barns covered with the bright green leaves, and even a few lumps that look like slow-moving people. (Anyone seen Aunt Adie Mae lately?) Kudzu has become a nuisance, but it does teach us a lesson. The mile-a-minute plant is a part of the South that reminds us of the dangers of moving too fast.

Like sweet, slow-brewed tea, Southern entertaining is about slowing down and taking time, no matter what. We Southerners have always known that entertaining is the one thing in life that is always appropriate. We may be going through a divorce (the fourth time), the plant might be closing down, we might be losing our mansion or our trailer, but no matter what, we can find something to celebrate with our loved ones. Hospitality is a Pearl Girl birthright, and we always love a party. With generosity and warmth, we'll get together for everything from a christening to a wake. We've gone to cocktail parties, ladies' lunches, barn dances, debutante teas, barbecues, bar and bat mitzvahs, clambakes, hoedowns, masquerades, covered dish suppers, and weddings. And I declare, we've even celebrated because it's Tuesday and we like our new shoes. Life is a joy, no matter what problems we face, and celebrating in the South is about keeping that joy alive.

Southern Tradition Is . . .

- **Honor**: *We don't cheat, lie, or embezzle.*
- **Courtesy**: *We call our elders Sir and Ma'am and always give up our seat to that pregnant lady.*
- **Place**: *We know where our kin are buried and who our neighbors are.*
- **The Soil**: *Even we city folks have a little garden with sweet, red tomatoes.*
- **Simplicity**: *We'd rather be laughing with friends than behind the ropes of a fancy club.*
- **Pride**: *Don't you dare insult our mamas.*
- **Respect**: *We won't say anything about your mama's housedress or cooking.*
- **Wisdom**: *We know that people are more valuable than things or ideas.*

Life is moving fast today, but there's no reason that we can't preserve our traditions. The South is still a place of good living, of pleasant people, of abundant dinners, and beautiful drives. Well, maybe not Atlanta or Charlotte at rush hour, but even we Southerners aren't perfect, honey.

Grandma's Silver (Family)

To us Southerners, Grandma's silver is a sacred thing handed down through the family. Those old patterns, burnished with a rich patina from the hands of friends and family, mean so much to us not because of what they're worth in dollars but because of what they're worth in our hearts. The silver is important because it symbolizes family. Not all families could afford silver, but all could afford traditions. From the cotton fields to the country clubs, we Southerners are all part of one family, and to us, family is everything. From our immediate to our extended family, we are all intertwined, and we grow roots wherever we go. Southerners know where their people came from and how they got there. They know where they lived, and where they were buried.

At a Southern party, you're likely to see not just neighbors and coworkers, but cousins and even parents. We want to surround ourselves with the people we love, and that means everyone from Granny to our Uncle Curtis, twice removed. To Pearl Girls, family love is the food that feeds our

Family Secrets

Leslie Anne Tarabella makes the best cookies you've ever tasted, but, sorry, sugah, I won't be telling you how they're made. A true Pearl Girl, Leslie Anne was sweet enough to share a batch of her famous cookies with me. She got her recipe from her great-grandmother in Hartselle, Alabama. When she was a little girl, Leslie Anne would make the cookies with Granny, and thinking about that beloved woman makes the cookies just a little bit sweeter in her mouth. When Leslie Anne taught school, she kept tradition alive by making the cookies in shapes for different holidays and sharing them with her students. Now that she has two boys of her own, she bakes the cookies whenever she can catch her breath!

After tasting these delicious treats, I asked Leslie Anne for the recipe, but to my surprise, she said that she couldn't divulge her secrets. This sweet young lady wanted to give me the recipe, but she was afraid she'd never hear the end of it. Her friends and family would be outraged if she shared such a sacred (and delicious) secret. Those cookies—and the secret recipe—were a proud family tradition, and she didn't want to share them with the world.

Well, Leslie Anne, as a real Pearl Girl, I'll hold on to that secret and the tradition behind it. Nothing's more important than family and tradition. Just try to make me a batch every once in a while!

souls, and we love to bring that family together (even that uncle who's a bit teched, bless his heart). Even when we throw a party and our family are not there, we like to behave as if they're looking over our shoulder—that's what makes us Pearl Girls the ladies that we are.

Southern entertaining begins in the home, and we Pearl Girls know that the best compliment we can receive is to be invited into the home of a new friend.

Pearl Girls know that it doesn't take fine china or the best linens to entertain, but it does take a bit of family and a lot of love. My mother never "entertained," so to speak. She was too busy making sure we had a roof over our heads and food on the table. Still, she entertained in other ways. Mother was an excellent seamstress, and she kept the young girls busy for hours telling them stories of her life while we sat there

Ten Southern Traditions We Can Keep Alive

1. *Setting a table, even with real cloth napkins, every day of the week*
2. *Sun hats and white gloves*
3. *Writing thank-you notes*
4. *Saying* sir *and* ma'am
5. *Giving a stranger a helping hand*
6. *Sitting on the porch and rocking for a spell*
7. *Slow-cooking greens all day long*
8. *Setting out the cheese straws (extra cayenne, please) and iced tea for company*
9. *Canning, quilting, and crocheting—our grandmothers did them to make do, but we can do them to make a home*
10. *Pearls, pearls, pearls*

watching her sew. It was her stories—and her love for and interest in us—that kept us quietly listening.

One of the ways we can hold on to tradition is to entertain the way our families did. In the past, people celebrated the season's bounty by sitting down together as family. Today it is far too easy to "drive through," order out, microwave freezer food, or call a caterer. We say we're way too busy and don't bother cooking the old way. If we don't hold on to tradition, though, it will slip away. Remember being at home, without the television and video droning, without little sister talking away on her cell phone, without music blaring from brother's room upstairs? Remember sitting together, smelling food cooking for hours, and that rich aroma swirling around the house? Remember baking fresh biscuits for breakfast and fresh rolls for dinner? The dining room is the heart of every Southern family.

The difference between today's and yesterday's world is that back then, we had to entertain ourselves—around the table and around the house—as families. We shared our lives and the lives of those we cared about and worshipped with. That may sound simple, but it seems harder and harder for us to do nowadays. Life is getting more complicated, but some things—a loving family, a warm home, a hearty supper—are as simple as they always were. That's still the bedrock of Southern entertaining. No matter how crazy anything else gets, we can always laugh and love together.

A PEARL GIRL KNOWS

E-mail has replaced letters. Television has replaced conversation. There will never be a replacement for home. Value your traditions and what you have learned from your family.

There's nothing like the smell of home. Our mothers baked, canned, and stewed all day long. When I have the time to do that, I do, but here's a quick recipe that gives me the smells and taste of an old family tradition without all the work.

Mama Liz's Shortcut Cobbler

> 1 stick of butter
> 1 cup of flour
> 1 cup of sugar
> 1 cup of milk
> 1 can of your favorite fruit

Melt the butter. Add the flour, the sugar, and the milk, and mix it all up good. Pour the mixture into a casserole. Pour the fruit over the mixture and bake at 350 degrees until done (or until it smells so good you can't wait!).

When we Pearl Girls entertain, we can hold on to the old ways, even if we're celebrating with friends rather than family. We can do it by treating those around us like family. (Well, not too much like family—don't pass around photos of your guests in their potty-training days.) We can do it by preserving the old recipes, by setting the table the way our mamas did, and most of all, keeping Southern hospitality alive. Southern hospitality means opening the door and saying, "Y'all come in—I'm pleased as punch to see you." We Pearl Girls still say that, and we still mean it. That's what Southern entertaining has always been about, and that's what it's still about today.

Keepsake Recipes

Sylvia, my mother-in-law, was the personification of Southern grace, dignity, and hospitality—in other words, a true Pearl Girl! She knew how to make everyone feel welcome in her home and could put on a spread fit for kings. Sylvia was one of those "cook by feel" Pearl Girls, able to put in a little of this and a little of that, and her guests always went home raving about her food and asking for her recipes.

One of my most treasured gifts from her is a keepsake book she gave me on my wedding day filled with recipes from many generations of my husband's family. With each recipe, she wrote a little about the family members and memories that made each dish special. Many of those relatives passed before I met them, but because of Sylvia's generosity and wit, I feel like I have a little bit of them here with me and some good home cookin', as well. One family favorite is from a very special aunt:

Aunt Dixie's Salad

> 1 large pack Jell-O (any flavor)
> 1 medium can crushed pineapple, with juice
> 2 cups buttermilk
> 2 cups Cool Whip

In a medium saucepan, heat the Jell-O and pineapple and juice to boiling. Remove the pan from the heat, and add the buttermilk. Pour the mixture into a bowl, and refrigerate until cool and thickened. Fold in the Cool Whip. Serves a gracious plenty!

—Darcy Crowder,
White, Georgia

Yes, darlin', in the South, Jell-O and Cool Whip are family traditions, and lots of family recipes use them! We Pearl Girls have always made do with what we had around, and making new traditions out of things that haven't been around for that long is part of our charm. We know that tradition isn't important just because it's old; it's important because it's handed down from the family that we love.

Christmas Oranges (Going Out of Our Way)

These days, we can hop on down to our local grocery store and buy everything from peanut brittle to death-by-chocolate cake, but there was a time when the typical Southern diet meant corn bread, greens, and peas. Sweet treats were rare, and they tasted all the better for it. There was nothing like waking up on Christmas morning and seeing a stocking full of nuts, hard candy, and, best of all, sweet, shining oranges. Now, a Florida Pearl Girl might not understand, but that sweet fruit was a taste of a faraway land, a special treat we waited for all year. Even in the leanest times, somehow our parents managed to get ahold of an orange for each child. Going out of our way to please others is something we learned early, and the taste of giving is as sweet in our mouths as it was back then.

How far will a Southern girl go for a good time? Any Southern gal worth her pearls knows that's a trick question—there's no such thing as going too far! Pearl Girls will drive across town for their guest's favorite flower. They'll spend hours making sure the roses on the cake are just so. They'll climb rickety ladders to make sure there's no dust on top of the armoire. They'll cook separate entrées for the vegetarian, the low-carber, and the guy who eats nothing but tuna fish. Their goal isn't to impress, and they're not obsessive-compulsive. (There's medicine for that.) Pearl Girls are women whose mothers taught them that making people at home is worth putting in the extra effort. They love their guests— even the old coots who never smile—and will do anything to make sure they have a good time. The secret to great Southern entertaining is not the etiquette. It's not our antique furniture or our crystal or even our stunning good looks

Fireside Chatters

As a new bride three thousand miles away from home, I was crying the blues until three officers' wives took me under their wings. I soon became a regular at many tea parties and cocktail hours. Carol, one of the officers' wives (and a great Pearl Girl), soon ascertained that my husband was right good for an upstart young preacher, and she held an intimate dinner party. That's what you did back then. You ascertained, and you entertained.

All the women arrived in our little black dresses, weighed down with whatever jewelry we could afford. We were ushered into the living room and served icy cold glasses of sweet tea and caviar on soya haystacks. Corn soya resembles magnified shredded wheat gone awry, and this is mixed with beaten sweetened egg whites. Little dollops of the mixture are baked until shiny as Christmas tree ornaments. Salty caviar makes the perfect contrast to these slightly sweet and crunchy little baskets.

Mind, these were the days before central air, or air of any kind for base housing, and the day was so steamy that even ambling to the refrigerator for sweet tea was considered a marathon. About halfway through one lap, we noticed a slight chill, and a draft too, coming from the doorway. Puzzled, we looked out to discover that the door was barricaded with huge tubs filled with ice, and Chuck was running back and forth checking the dozens of fans blowing gales of icy wind our way.

Carol had decided that I needed a roaring fireplace to chase away the blues—even in the middle of summer. And no expense or trouble would be spared to make sure that I had the perfect party! Everything was well chilled—including us!—and by the time we settled down in the living room for dessert, the fire was roaring away. And that's when the sky darkened and the wind whipped up. Within minutes, the temperature

Continued...

(though we Southern gals sure got those, sugar). It's that we love being around people and making them happy.

Southern girls are crazy about having a good time, even if it means being, well, a little crazy. Crazy to go the extra mile. Crazy to give a helping hand. Most of all, crazy to make sure that each and every person enjoys themselves. Southern hospitality is about rolling out the red carpet and giving each guest the royal treatment, whether he lives in a mansion or a tar-paper shack.

Champagne (Bringing in the New Sparkle)

Southerners know how to make the best darned sweet tea you ever tasted, but they also know when to break out the bubbly. Champagne is a bit of sophistication that livens up our traditional celebrations. We aren't giving up that delicious tea (and a touch of *white lightning* when we're in the mood), but we are bringing in a bit of sparkle, class, and glitz to liven up our grits. We love doing things the way our mamas did—so we have the rules of etiquette down pat and we know how to use them—but we also love the best of the new.

Here in the South, we've got the gracious old plantations along the Natchez Trace, but we've also got the golf courses of Alabama's Robert Trent Jones Trail; we've got the rolling bluegrass of Kentucky, but we've also got the bright lights of Houston; we've got old-fashioned gospel choirs, but we also have pastors who play the electric guitar. We love tradition, and we love doing things the way our families have done them for years, but we know how to bring in what's best of the new. And when you think about it, there was a time when even corn bread in an iron skillet and smothered pork chops were innovations. Thank goodness our grandmothers weren't afraid to try something new, because, I declare, I don't want to face a world without gumbo!

One difference between the South and the rest of the country is that we know how to incorporate the new without steam-rolling over our past (though, sad to say, sometimes it doesn't feel that way). Just because we're watching our figures and our

A Civil War Feast

Southerners have always gone all out to make sure their guests have a good time. Mary Chesnut, a famous American Civil War diarist, writes about the Christmas dinner her hosts prepared for her during the middle of the war. In spite of the war's privations, everyone went out of their way to make the holiday the best. Mary wore her best dress from Paris (from before the war, of course). Her hosts served oyster soup, roast mutton, boned turkey, wild duck, partridge, plum pudding, sauterne, burgundy, sherry, and Madeira. Whew, honey, and I was thinking baking my own Christmas cake is going all out!

cholesterol count doesn't mean that we have to give up delicious food—we just adapt and learn to make it in new ways. (And when we really want to celebrate, we know that we can sometimes still bring out that good old fatback and salty ham.)

When it comes to Southern entertaining, some things have changed for the better, as well. We're bringing Latin and Asian flavors into our cooking. Women are still dressing to the

Southern Entertaining— Yesterday and Today

CLASSIC	NEW
Fried catfish	Sushi
Pickled peaches	Salsa
String quartet	New country
Spoon bread	Polenta
Boiled greens	Field greens
Steeplechase	NASCAR
Mint julep	Margarita
Ham and biscuits	Prosciutto and melon
Pearls	Pearls, of course!

New-Style Wilted Lettuce

Wilted lettuce was always a mouthwatering treat in the old days. Some folks called it "killed" lettuce, though it tasted pretty lively on the tongue. That might sound a bit strange to outsiders, but you've never tasted anything so good.

Here's how you make it: Tear up some lettuce and mix it in a sturdy bowl with a little vinegar (just plain old cider vinegar is good for this recipe), a touch of mustard, a dash of sugar and some pepper. Then cook up a big old batch of bacon, and pour that hot fat right over the greens. Delicious!

To save your arteries, you can make the same recipe, but leave out the bacon. Go ahead and tear up those greens, and mix them with your seasonings. (Add some salt this time, since you won't have that delicious, salty bacon fat.) Add a dash of dark soy sauce or balsamic vinegar to give it a little richness. Heat up some olive oil in a pan, and use it to sauté some shallots, green onions, or some mushrooms. Pour this hot mixture over your greens. It may not be Mama's recipe, but it's a touch of the new with a taste of the old . . . the Pearl Girl way.

nines (thank goodness), but now they can wear pantsuits along with their pearls. We have imported flowers to mix with the beautiful azaleas and gardenias in our gardens. We have French and even Australian wines along with our iced tea.

The secret to welcoming new things is not to throw out the old ones. Just because we're eating sushi doesn't mean we have to give up fried catfish. Just because we decorate with a new flat-screen TV doesn't mean we have to give up Mama's sideboard. Just because we listen to Shania Twain doesn't mean we have to give up Hank Williams Sr. A little touch of glitz livens up the grits, but we Pearl Girls know that the grits are always there in our hearts.

Excuses to Throw a Party, Southern Style, Any Time of Year

Everyone knows that we Pearl Girls don't need an excuse to throw a party—every day is a party for us! But here are a few good reasons to gather together friends and family.

January

- *Elvis Presley's Birthday (January 8).* Celebrate the King's birthday with Memphis-style barbecue (or one of those fried peanut butter and banana sandwiches), and boogie all night long.
- *Robert E. Lee's Birthday (January 19).* Although he despised slavery, Robert E. Lee, arguably the greatest general of the Civil War, decided to fight for his home state of Virginia in the war. Honor his memory by preparing a pre–Civil War meal (slow-cooked greens, corn bread, and ham), and make a toast to a real Southern gentleman.
- *Martin Luther King Jr. Day (third Monday in January).* Use the day to teach your children about the man who fought to make us all free—read his "I Have a Dream" speech or portions of "Letter from a Birmingham Jail."

February

- *Mardi Gras (the day before Lent).* Laissez les bons temps rouler! Mix up some high-octane drinks, pull out those masks and beads, and let it all hang out with a few dozen of your closest friends. And don't forget some good old Nawlins jazz to set the mood.

- Who Needs Valentine's Day Party (February 14). For those of us in between sweethearts, Valentine's Day can be anything but a celebration. Invite your single friends over for gossip, cocktails, and a couple of good videos. Who needs a man when we've got such wonderful Pearl Girls for friends?

March

- Garden Party (spring) When the weather turns in your corner of the world, welcome the ladies over for a real Southern garden party. Hats, gloves, and your best flowered dress are the order of the day. Cucumber sandwiches and petits fours are on the menu. (A good rule of thumb is that if your significant other finds it too sissy, it's perfect garden party fare.) Don't forget the iced tea and the gossip, and your party is sure to succeed.
- Cherry Blossom Festival (varies by region). Washington, D.C., and other Southern cities celebrate a cherry blossom festival, but you can have one of your own. Decorate your house or garden with cherry blossoms (real or paper), cook up some light spring fare (asparagus and ham, tender green salad, and lemon pie), and give everyone an excuse to wear their pretty new spring clothes.

April

- Pascua Florida Day (April 2). On this day in 1513, Ponce de Leon sighted Florida and named it Pascua Florida. Two weeks later, pioneering developers broke ground on the first retirement condo. Waste away in Margaritaville, or just serve a key lime pie, in honor of our very own Redneck Riviera.
- Tax Day (April 15). Throw a frugal party of chicken and

dumplings and the cheapest beer to mourn the money wasted on government pork, or go all the way with champagne and caviar before the tax man takes it away.

- San Jacinto Day (April 19). Put on them boots and cook up some chili, pardner. It's time to honor the birth of the Republic of Texas. Sing "The Yellow Rose of Texas" in honor of all those cowgirl Pearl Girls.

May

- Kentucky Derby (first Saturday in May). Mix up some mint juleps and whip up some ham biscuits. Gambling is optional; hats are not.
- Memphis Barbecue Cook-Off (midmonth). This Super Bowl of Swine is the largest pork barbecue cook-off in the world. If you can't make it, pick up some local stuff, roll up your sleeves, and dig in. (Some things are so good, even we Pearl Girl ladies can use our fingers!)
- Vidalia Onion Festival (mid-May). They say Vidalia onions are so sweet, you can bite into them like an apple, but we Pearl Girls should refrain unless we have a whole lot of mouthwash nearby. Invite your friends over for a sweet onion covered-dish, and have everything from onion casserole to onion bread. Just remember, kiss your sweetie only if he's been eating onions, too!
- Mecklenburg Independence Day (May 20). Don't wait until July to celebrate our independence from the British. In 1775, Mecklenburg County (in present-day North Carolina), declared its independence, and Charlotte has been celebrating its own independence day ever since. So get out those flags and sparklers a little early this year, and celebrate American freedom in May!
- Indy 500 (events throughout May). It might take place in Indiana, but the Indy 500 has a special place in the Southern heart. Follow

the events throughout the month; then invite over everyone on the big race day. Beer (or soda for the teetotaler) and a whole lot of hollering are the order of the day.

June

- *Flag Day* (June 14). Here in the South, we fly our flags proudly. Decorate your home or yard in red, white, and blue, and display your true colors. Invite your family and neighbors for an all-American (and all-Southern) meal, and top it off with a white cake decorated with red strawberries and blue blueberries. Play some patriotic music, and celebrate the flag we fly to honor our country.
- *Juneteenth* (June 19). Make a picnic, and gather together the family. Juneteenth celebrates the word of freedom reaching Southern slaves. Long celebrated among African Americans in the South, the popularity of this day is spreading.
- *Watermelon Thump* (last full weekend in June). The good folks of Luling, Texas, have been holding their watermelon thump for more than fifty years. Invite the whole gang for watermelon-eating and seed-spitting contests. (As a real Pearl Girl, you might want to leave these to the kids—a faceful of watermelon ruins your makeup.) Serve up cookout fare and, if you choose, a spiked watermelon for the grown-ups.
- *Catching June Bugs* (whenever they show up, honey). When I was a child, catching june bugs was one of the best sports of summer. We'd tie a string to one of the beetle's legs and watch it fly around like our own personal helicopter. Those critters can escape unharmed in the end, but if your kids are worried, fly a kite together, and celebrate the beginning of our Southern summer.

July

- Green Corn Festival (traditionally, when green corn appears; sometime in June or July). A centuries-old Cherokee holiday celebrating the first corn harvest of the year. Hot corn pones, corn soup, spoon bread, corn relish . . . Celebrate with your favorite corn dishes. Traditionally, it was a dancing and storytelling time, so turn the lights down low (or better yet, build a bonfire) and share your favorite stories (from your imagination or from books) together as a family.
- Red Neck Games (mid-July). This East Dublin, Georgia, answer to the 1996 Olympic Games in Atlanta features the mud-pit flop, watermelon-seed spitting, hubcap hurl, and big hair contest. Feel free to host some games of your own, but remember—a real Pearl Girl would never go bobbing for pigs' feet.
- Ice Cream Churning (all month). Celebrate national ice cream month with an old-fashioned ice cream churning. Invite all your neighbors, borrow a couple of extra churns, and make up a few batches of your different flavors—vanilla, peach, and go crazy with new combinations like banana-chocolate or pistachio-cherry. With some hot fudge and caramel on the side (and liquors like crème de menthe and Kahlúa for the big folks), you'll be the most popular person on the block.

August

- Catfish Fry (we need a whole month for catfish, sugah!). August is national catfish month. Bread some of these with corn meal and a little cayenne; then invite your friends and family over for the South's favorite fried fish. Add some homemade coleslaw, watermelon, and peach cobbler, and you've got a little piece of heaven on a plate.

- Family Reunion (whenever you can drag them all together). With school still out and the weather hot, August is the month to get your family together in the great outdoors. Find a local park, drag out those horseshoes and that old croquet set, and get the whole family, including those cousins you never seem to see, for some old-fashioned picnic fare and lighthearted games.
- Sorority Rush (varies by school). Whether they pledged Chi-O or Tri-Delt, we Southern gals giggled, cried, and hugged together during our own sorority rushes. Hold your daughter's hand (ever since we graduated from college, Southern mothers have been waiting for this week) or relive the parties with your girlfriends. Dust off that old pin, dig out those song lyrics, and spend an evening with the women who'll be your sisters for life.

September

- Football, football, football (varies by team). Celebrate the rites of the South's other religion by donning the colors from head to toe and cheering for your team. There are fewer weddings during each state's football rivalry week. (No Southern girl would make her guests choose between her and the Georgia–Georgia Tech game.) Whether it's the local high school or your alma mater, gather together your fellow fans and scream till you're hoarse.
- Miss America Pageant (mid-month). Sure, the pageant is held in New Jersey, but we Pearl Girls have made it our own. Invite over your girlfriends, cheer for your favorites, and critique those gowns. And don't forget your tiara—every Pearl Girl deserves a crown!

- *Boll Weevil Festival (end of the month). Pay tribute to the pest that ended large-scale cotton production in the South. The citizens of Enterprise, Alabama, have erected a monument to the critter, and have this annual festival in his honor. You may not think of celebrating a bug, but those pretty little Pearl Girl hands don't have to be pickin' cotton thanks to him.*

- *Hunt Breakfast (varies depending on hunting season). Get together your friends and family for your heartiest Southern breakfast for after the predawn hunt: biscuits, country sausage and gravy, fried apples, and (naturally) grits. Welcome those hunters home (even if they didn't bag anything but a couple of tall tales), or just put on your orange cap and skip the hunt altogether—we won't tell if you won't.*

- *Pumpkin Carving (last week in October). Get those ghosts and goblins ready for Halloween with a pumpkin-carving contest. Have your guests bring pumpkins, and you can supply knives, bowls, and lots of newspaper. Warm everyone up with some hot cocoa and home-baked cookies, and give out small prizes for the best (and worst) carving.*

November

- *Wurstfest (late October to early November). The best of the wurst! In 1845, a group of German settlers came to New Braunfels, Texas, and their descendants still celebrate their German heritage today with music, food, and dancing. You can get your sausage Texas-style in a wurst taco. To celebrate at home, pick up some good German beer, and cook up a bratwurst.*

- *Sadie Hawkins Day (November 17). Invite your girlfriends for an adult-style Sadie Hawkins dance. Southern girls love to let men* know they care with a bat of the eyelash and a flip of the hair, but sometimes just coming out and asking that cute guy in the next cubicle can be just as much fun.

- Pie-Baking Party (the week before the fourth Thursday in November). Originally a Yankee holiday (in typical Yankee fashion, it was moved from the fifth to the fourth Thursday in November to extend the shopping season), Thanksgiving has become a Southern tradition. Get your friends together a couple of days before the holiday, and whip up some pies. If your oven isn't big enough, enlist the help of your neighbors. You can do your part to make the holiday about togetherness and thankfulness, and less about the first days of the shopping season.

December

- Ornament-Making Party (two to three weeks before Christmas). Everyone has a Christmas party, so try something a bit different this year. Visit a craft store for ideas and supplies, and don't forget women's magazines, which give lots of suggestions. If you or your friends are Jewish, painting wooden dreidels (available already made at some craft stores) makes a great craft, as well. Have projects in mind for both little and big hands. Serve your guests cider and finger foods, or a healthy lunch after the crafts are finished.

CHAPTER 2

The Good Hostess

We make a living by what we get, we make a life by what we give.
—SIR WINSTON CHURCHILL

I'm tired of playing worn-out depressing ladies in frayed bathrobes. I'm going to get a new hairdo and look terrific and go back to school and even if nobody notices, I'm going to be the most fulfilled lady on the block.
—JOANNE WOODWARD
    THOMASVILLE, GEORGIA
    (AND HOLLYWOOD, CALIFORNIA)

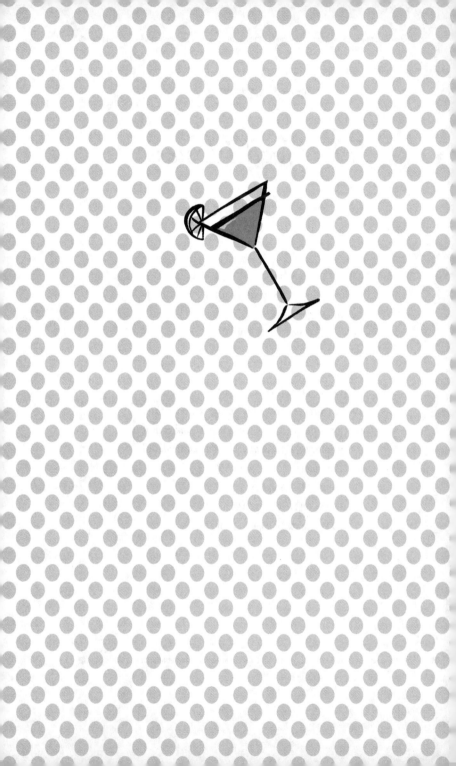

S HE ANSWERS THE DOOR WITH A SMILE, HANDS YOU A cool drink, and somehow gets you started on a conversation with a handsome man in the corner you wouldn't have had the courage to speak to otherwise. In other words, a good hostess always makes you feel comfortable right away. A real Pearl Girl knows that the star of any party is the hostess, and she's always ready to shine.

The Heart of the Art

Hospitality is at the heart of Southern tradition. We may not always be happy to have so many visitors (just ask anyone on I-285 at rush hour), but we've always been warm and welcoming, and we've done all we can to make sure that they felt special under our watch. Southern girls know how to turn on the charm, and we do it with the same warmth and caring whether we're talking to a multimillionaire or an auto mechanic. We're all God's creatures, after all, and we love everyone (even the woman who can't remember our name after we've been introduced to her five times, bless her heart).

Southern girls know that the heart of the art of hostessing is selflessness and caring. Whether she is a full-time homemaker or works outside the home (and is probably still a full-time homemaker!), a Southern woman's first thought is other people. Even when she's under a deadline at work and making four pies for the school's bake sale, she still makes sure her family has a hot meal (even if occasionally it comes ready-made from the grocery store). Pearl Girls want, above all else, to make their families happy. So when they entertain, they think of their guests as family, too.

Goodness Gracious!

In Colonial America, pineapples were a symbol of luxury and abundance. If a hostess could provide a pineapple to display on her table, it showed that she must be a wealthy, or at least resourceful, housewife, so trade in the fruit was brisk. In fact, pineapples were so much in demand that they were sometimes rented for a day's use.

Southern girls want to welcome friends and neighbors into their homes because they want to share the love that they have there. We Pearl Girls are homebodies at heart. That doesn't mean that we're wallflowers (we love to laugh and dance with the best of them), but it does mean that our hospitality comes from wanting to share our homes, and ourselves, with others.

The Goodness in the Graciousness

A real Pearl Girl knows that having open hearts and open homes brings that happiness back to us. The more we welcome people, the better our homes become. We don't hide

---

Five Ways to Share Our Famous Hospitality

1. *Welcome new neighbors with a home-baked casserole. If they're still unpacking from the move, supply paper plates and forks, as well.*
2. *Keep a few appetizers in your freezer for quick heating, so that when drop-in guests arrive, you can welcome them like you cooked all day.*
3. *Stock your guest room like the finest hotel. Supply travel-size soaps, shampoos, and mouthwash, bottled water, local maps, and light snacks. Your guests will feel welcomed and pampered.*
4. *On holidays, don't forget the people who work to make your life easier. Give a little something to your mail carrier and your garbage collector to let them know you value their hard work.*
5. *Smile, smile, smile! That fabulous Pearl Girl smile will bring brightness into someone else's day (and you'll look a whole lot prettier).*

Aunt Pearl's
Perfect Peach Cobbler

It was 10 a.m. on a Saturday morning, and that meant that it was time for Mama to call up MaryLou at the Curl Up and Dye for their usual gossip exchange. "I have exactly four hours to prepare for the Collilo girl and her Yankee clan," Mama said. My older brother had knocked our socks off with his engagement to Mary Collilo, a girl from New York City. As soon as she got over the shock, Mama picked herself up off the living room floor and began planning an "informal get-together." That informal get-together would feature two meats, five side vegetables, fresh biscuits, iced tea, and, of course, the crowning glory, the perfect peach cobbler.

"You know how those Yankee folks are, MaryLou," she continued, "they're all wrapped up in their fancy restaurants and their take-out food. I bet those Collilo folks never tasted a good home-cooked meal. I've been cooking all morning—I even have the perfect crust made." Just then, Mama gasped, "Where are the peaches? I can't make Aunt Pearl's perfect peach cobbler without the peaches! Honey, run over to Beulah's and see if she has any peaches."

Well, I ran to Beulah's as fast as my little legs could carry me. When I got there, Beulah was on her hands and knees poking around a cabinet. "Oh, honey, I'm glad to see you. How can I peel those peaches without my peeler? Your mama brought over a bag of peaches for Aunt Pearl's perfect peach cobbler yesterday, but MaryLou was visiting last night and must have taken my peeler."

In a blink of an eye, Beulah, I, and a big bag of peaches squeezed into her truck and cruised into town to MaryLou's shop. Her husband, Bud, was staring at a head full of curlers and trying to figure out how to take them out. "MaryLou's upstairs messing with something in the kitchen. Anyone know how these things work?"

We rushed upstairs with no time to answer. MaryLou was standing with a bowl full of peach pie filling. "I'm glad to see you. Your mama asked me to make Aunt Beulah's perfect peach cobbler, but in all the excitement, I forgot to make the pastry." I grabbed MaryLou's hand, and everybody got in the truck, bag of peaches, bowl of filling, and all.

When we got home, Mama was standing over her empty pie crust. We looked at the dish, the filling, and the peaches. In the confusion, Mama had forgotten she'd asked two friends to make the cobbler, and she started making it herself. And even with all that help, we still didn't have a cobbler! Mama grabbed the filling, dumped it into the pastry she had made, and put it into the warm oven. "Looks like I was intent on having this cobbler today!" Mama laughed. "I hope they appreciate it."

Three hours later, Mary Collilo and family arrived, and she handed Mama a fresh apple pie. "Our hotel had a kitchenette, so Mother and I whipped up some homemade apple pie this morning. I hope you don't mind."

Mama showed a bit of true Southern hospitality (or maybe relief that her boy was marrying a girl, New Yorker or not, with some good manners of her own). She smiled and took the dish. "How thoughtful of you. I hadn't even thought about dessert!"

—Jennifer Jabaley
  Blue Ridge, Georgia

ourselves away. Instead, we take the Bible's teaching seriously and know that if we spend our talents well, by giving them to friends and families, they'll return to us twentyfold.

Goodness Gracious!

Psychologists in America and Germany have shown that making a facial expression alters our mood. If we make an angry face, our heart rate shoots up. If we smile, we find life much funnier. A Pearl Girl could have told you this without a lot of expensive studies or fancy degrees! We always keep a smile on our faces, and we know that it makes us (and those around us) much happier.

Being gracious is an art that anyone, whether she's shy and bookish or the life of the party, can share with others. We might tell a story that keeps a room in stitches, we might bake a batch of brownies and quietly bring them to the office, we might throw on a little black number and strut so the whole world can enjoy our beauty, or we visit that old Mr. Johnson, who attended our church until he got too sick. It's the Southern way, it's the Pearl Girl way, and it's a tradition worth keeping alive.

Draw Them In . . . Again and Again

Being a good hostess is like being in love—you are always thinking about other people, and about how to make them happy. The basic element of being a good hostess is not the

Open Hearts and Open Tables

The South is well known for its friendliness and hospitality. When we meet someone on the street, we greet him with a kind word or a smile. We give these little things freely to one another to brighten the day.

This Southern trait extends to helping someone who needs assistance. Many years ago, a family, including two young children, had a flat tire near our house. My husband went out to lend a helping hand. This happened around midday—dinner time as we say in the South—and I had lunch on the table. I had prepared fried chicken in an iron skillet, green beans, mashed potatoes, sliced tomatoes, corn bread, brownies, and iced tea.

When the spare tire was finally on the car, my husband remarked that it was time to eat. He casually extended an invitation, and it was gladly accepted. Needless to say, I did not have food left over for a meal that night as I had planned, but I was grateful to be able to help them.

—Marie Ursery
Piney Chapel, Alabama

Mrs. Ursery was not just a warm, hospitable Southern hostess, she was my English teacher back in school. When I think of her, I always think of diagramming sentences—but maybe now I'll think of skillet-baked corn bread. She's a great teacher and a real lady, and I'm proud to know her.

> *There are about the same percentages of amusing, gifted, humorous, boring, stingy, and malicious people in every social drawer.... Life is too short—plant and tend a friendship garden that will grow and flourish.*
>
> —EMILY WHALEY
> PINOPOLIS,
> SOUTH CAROLINA

quality of her silver, the deliciousness of her food, or even her good looks—it's her conversation. No matter what other entertainment you arrange for your guests, conversation is the basic ingredient. You can deliver beautiful things and a beautiful setting, but it is ultimately the people you have at your party who will draw your guests back again and again.

Making sure that your party has great conversation begins with your guest list. Now, when you're inviting over family, you don't have much choice, and a Pearl Girl would never suggest that you don't invite your uncle because he enjoys sitting in a chair with some chaw rather than making conversation, or your cousin just because he's more interested in his Nintendo than in his family. For them, smile and try to draw them out as best you can, and if you can't, let them be. If you're inviting friends and neighbors, though, you have more choice, and you should keep in mind that a compatible group of people will have a great time.

A PEARL GIRL KNOWS

A Southern hostess always remembers names. If she forgets, though, it's no problem. No Pearl Girl ever minded being called sugah, dah'lin, or sweetheart!

Your guests are the most important part of your party, and a good hostess must know how to tend to them. You can start even before the date of your party by sending a personal note letting them know how much you're looking forward to seeing them. The minute they walk in the door, greet them with a hug (or a firm handshake or, if you are close to a person, with a kiss). Just remember that if you kiss a husband, you definitely have to also kiss his wife!

Everybody should have one great story or joke in reserve to share when things get quiet, but you don't have to go to the lengths I did to get it. When I found out I needed a cervical fusion (that is an anterior cervical fusion—meaning the incision has to be made on the front of my neck!!), my ex-husband (Bless His Heart # 2), Danny Michael, was the surgeon. Danny is not only a wonderful surgeon, he is the father of my daughters. I was confident he would do a good job, however, I was even more confident this would make a good story (especially at a party!) I knew I was right as soon as I was wheeled into the operating room. You should have seen the looks on the faces of the nurses and the other doctors when they learned that my ex was the man with the knife in his hand!

—Deborah Ford
Birmingham, Alabama

Conversing with your guests is an art that we Pearl Girls learn first in our families. We learn on our mothers' knees that being genuinely interested in those around us is the secret to great conversation. Every etiquette book will tell you to ask questions about the other person, but we Pearl Girls know that just asking is not good enough. You have to listen, and the rest will follow.

Ask a guest questions about himself. This doesn't mean playing a game of twenty questions. (Where do you work? Do you have kids? Where'd you go to school?) Ask that way, and pretty soon your guest will wonder if he's at a party or an interview. Instead, ask one or two questions; then really listen to the answer. If your guest went to Auburn, follow up by asking when they're going to beat 'Bama. If your guest has grandkids, ask if they did anything cute recently. The key is actually caring what you hear, and caring is what we Pearl Girls are all about.

SOUTHERN TRANSLATION

precious [presh´ əs] adj. *in the North, something valuable, such as a gem; in the South, a glorious gem of a girl.*

Every good hostess knows that there's an art not just in talking with people, but in getting them to talk to each other. When you introduce your guests, give them a tidbit that they have in common. You'll have to know your guests pretty well to do this, which can be hard at a large gathering, so think about who you're inviting before the party starts. See if you can list two or three things about each guest—where do they work, do they have hobbies, are they married, do they have children. Then when the party starts, you'll have an easier time getting conversation started. "Mr. Smith, meet Mr. Johnson" won't get any wallflower into a conversation. But "Mr. Smith, meet Mr. Johnson. Did you know that Mr. Smith went to Florida State, and Mr. Johnson went to the University of Florida?" Since you're inviting gentlemen, with any luck a spirited sports conversation, and not a fistfight, will break out.

You don't have to be to the manner born to be a true belle. Just ask Kathy Burns. Kathy came from a hardworking Southern family. "The closest thing to silver in my family was the lid of a mason jar," she says of her upbringing. "I didn't have the money or the time for a social sorority in college. . . . I was too busy working forty hours a week and being a full-time student. I was the first person in my family to go to college. I always envied the girls who 'came out' in their white cotillion gowns, the girls who giggled with their sorority sisters and wore their pins with pride, the ladies who wore hats and gloves and went to lunch and tea. I wanted a mansion and a hoop skirt—I wanted to be Scarlett."

Kathy wanted to come from high cotton, but the closest her family got was the cotton mill. But like any true Pearl Girl, Kathy didn't let a little thing like that stop her, and she created the character of Mary Margret Smythe (of the Georgia Smythes, sugah). When Kathy paints on her Mary Margret face and pulls on those white gloves, she becomes a true belle. Mary Margret epitomizes the high-class Southern lady: "She has been in search of the golden hoop skirt since the age of twelve, when she completed the catechism of belles taught by three generations of females in her family, chose her silver pattern, purchased her first pair of white pumps, and got a hope chest for Christmas. She carries a pocketbook, uses an icebox that contains only Hellmann's mayonnaise, has an entire cookbook devoted to funeral casseroles using cream of mushroom soup and Velveeta cheese, and still calls her father Daaaaaddy."

Kathy knew attitude made a belle, so she went ahead and made herself into Mary Margret. Now she travels throughout the South playing the character. And she has the attitude to carry it off in the Pearl Girl way. When she dies, her friends will say, "She was sooooo

Continues . . .

precious. She lived her life to the fullest . . . survivin', endurin', and sufferin' with such grace, dignity, and style."

Says Mary Margret, "In order to discuss Southern belles, we must talk about the legend, the legacy, and the laughter. Just for a moment look at my life—my deviled egg plate broke, my daughter joined the marines, my son is taking ballet lessons, my husband is being transferred to Michigan, my doctor says I have to give up iced tea, my Chi O legacy daughter wants to be a Tri Delta. . . . What's a belle to do? I think I'll call up Grandma and take her to lunch!"

If you're really worried that your guests won't be able to make conversation, for instance, you're having a block party in a brand-new neighborhood and nobody knows anyone else, help them along by making it a game. Give each guest a list of tidbits about the various guests: ran track in college, owns an electronics store, has been to Europe five times. The first guest to match the tidbits with names receives a special gift, and the rest of your guests will go home with a list of new friends.

Being Bellefied

A Southern hostess knows that she is the star of the party. That is, unless she's hosting a wedding, though a real Southern girl knows that the mother of the bride is the one that should be congratulated. The hostess chooses the guests, provides the food, sets the mood, and is the star of the show! There's a reason that so many Pearl Girls, from Tallulah Bankhead on down to Reese Witherspoon, have been famous

Momma's Pearls

Why, then the world's mine oyster,
Which I with sword will open.

—William Shakespeare,
The Merry Wives of Windsor

My granny and nana didn't have much choice about their pearls;
they came in lovely strands. The world was my momma's oyster; it
just took her a long time to realize it. I think she's always wished she
had known sooner. I know the world is my oyster, have always
known, but it has frequently felt overwhelming and impossible rather
than promising. I've lacked confidence and been indecisive in finding
my pearl. The limitless has been limiting. I want my daughter to see
and believe that the world is a place where pearls are hers for the tak-
ing; I want her to take a sword, pry the oyster open, and know ex-
actly what to do with the pearl she finds.

—Laura Lefler
Knoxville, Tennessee

Laura Lefler is a Pearl Girl who knows what it takes to be a belle—
attitude! And like any true Pearl Girl, she looks to her mother for in-
spiration, and to her daughter for hope.

actresses. We love being center stage. There's a bit of Hollywood actress in all Pearl Girls, and playing hostess is the time to let it shine!

Being the center of your party means being "bellefied," and being bellefied means knowing how to be a star, inside and out. A Pearl Girl knows that true beauty and a pleasing presentation starts from within, and we also know that confidence is the most compelling element of true beauty. A belle looks the best that she can with what she's given, and because of her inner beauty, she looks far better than the sum of her parts. She might have crow's-feet, cellulite, a sagging tummy, and an oversize nose, but there's something about her that can shine, even without surgery (though there's nothing wrong with a little nip and tuck). You don't have to spend a lot of money to be bellefied, but you do have to do everything you can to look your best. Bellefied is not just dia-

Rules for Being a Southern Belle

1. Dresses like a lady, not a lady of the night.
2. Keeps a smile on her face that could melt the heart of an IRS agent.
3. Is always ready to share the news (but keeps the family secrets).
4. Keeps everything shipshape: penmanship, fellowship, stewardship.
5. Lets a gentleman be a gentleman by allowing him to open a door for her, thank you very much.

monds and pearls from head to toe. It can be dime-store sunglasses and rubber flip-flops. The secret is attitude.

The Pearl Girl attitude means that wherever she is, whatever she has to do, and whenever she has to do it, the belle can handle the situation, and she can do it with grace. A Southern belle knows who she is, and knows what she can be. Southern girls are no different than any other women in the world—we're working with the same wrinkles and the same droopy parts—the difference is that we take what we have and let it shine!

How to Prevent Being Outblonded

No matter what color hair she has, a real Southern hostess is always a blonde in her heart. She's gorgeous, and she's the center of attention, meaning that she's never going to be outblonded. Pearl Girls know that it is what's inside that counts, but that doesn't mean that we let the outside fall apart!

We take care of our bodies, our faces, our clothes, but most important, our hair! It's part of our hair-i-tage! Whatever our hair color, though, we don't ever want to be outblonded when we entertain. Blonde is an attitude, and we Southern girls know how to carry it off.

SOUTHERN TRANSLATION

Outblonded [out bländ´ ed] **n.** *the state of being outdressed, outshone, out-thought, or outlasted by another woman. If she's a bigger sensation, you've been outblonded, honey!*

Pearl Girls never leave home looking like "Hope digging potatoes!" First and foremost, a Pearl Girl takes care of her skin, applies discreet and appropriate makeup, and wears clean, well-maintained clothes. (And we listen to our mothers and always wear clean underwear—you never know when you're going to be in an accident, especially if you drive like me!) Not being outblonded is the heart of simplicity: comb your hair, stick on that lip gloss, put on your sunglasses (and if you don't have time to do your hair, a hat), hold your head high, and have a great day.

Looking good doesn't have to cost a mint. (My two best accessories are two old pearl collars that I bought at an antique shop—they each cost ten dollars.) Choose a few classic pieces (don't forget that little black dress, honey!); then dress them up with something unique. If you can't afford scarves and shoes from a fancy boutique, don't worry! Get yourself down to your local consignment and second-hand stores. You'll find costume jewelry, scarves, jackets, and everything you need to play dress up, some of it never worn! Remember what it felt like to wear your mama's heels and gloves? A little bit of creative shopping will let you feel that way every day, and you don't have to be a millionaire to do it. That's what being a blonde, and a Pearl Girl, is all about.

A Pearl Girl knows that being overdressed is always better than being underdressed. But remember, when choosing your clothes, always be a lady and watch those neck- and hemlines. As Mammy said to Miss Scarlett, a lady doesn't show her bosom before three o'clock!

SOUTHERN TRANSLATION

streaking [strēk´ iŋ] n. *in the Northern United States, taking off one's clothes and running around nekkid as a fool; in the Southern United States, adding blonde highlights to one's hair.*

A Pearl Girl doesn't just care for her clothes; she also cares for her body (especially that shining hair). Gone are the days when a lady didn't break a sweat. (Well, we Pearl Girls still don't really sweat—we glisten.) We still indulge in fried chicken and sweet potato pie, but we spend time working it off (and bringing out that pretty blush in our cheeks).

If you want to be a blonde literally (and not just in your attitude), make sure you have the time and the money. If you are brunette or anything darker, you'll be spending a lot of time at the hairdresser keeping up those roots. Now, we Pearl Girls love having some time to share the news with our best friend and psychiatrist (otherwise known as our hairdresser), but we don't need a second mortgage on the house to pay for it. Just be sure if you do go blonde, you're ready for the commitment. (A beauty shop is like an auto repair shop—it's all about the maintenance.) And always remember the fade factor. Sun, pollutants, and frequent shampooing strip the color and shine from that "flirt alert" hair. Wait at least twenty-four hours between shampooing (and forty-eight hours is even better), use tepid (not hot) water (better for that complexion, too!), and use a special shampoo for color-treated hair.

A PEARL GIRL KNOWS

If you're going to get your teeth capped, be sure the new additions don't look like Chiclets!

—Kate Macleod Michael
Central Florida

Goodness Gracious!

Until 1879, crude curling irons heated over the fire were the only method of bringing a wave to those flat locks. That year, Marcel Grateau invented a gadget that produced the marcel wave. In 1906, a German stylist developed an expensive (and often painful) twelve-hour process called the permanent wave. We Pearl Girls don't need to go through pain for a permanent wave, honey—we've already got our hands flapping!

Never Too Much of a Good Thing!

I was at a cocktail party in the North, wondering when I could make my escape, when I met a man from Massachusetts. When I told him I was originally from Georgia, he smiled in delight. "I'm from a family of jewelry dealers," he said, "and that's my favorite part of the country." Whenever his family gets a large, jewel-studded piece, they send it to their buyers in the South. These buyers are always begging for bigger, better (and did I say bigger?) pieces, and the jewelers are more than happy to oblige.

One time, those Massachusetts boys decided to play a joke on their Southern buyers. They had purchased a piece at an estate sale, and they thought that absolutely no one would want it. It was a gold bracelet, several inches high and secured by a clasp. The bracelet was so large that it looked more like a piece of armor than a piece of jewelry. Every inch was studded by precious or semiprecious stones and curlicues of gold. The jewelry dealers laughed as they packed it up, thinking that they'd be getting it right back to use as a curiosity piece. Instead, they received a call almost as soon as the courier delivered the package. "Where'd you get that gorgeous thing?" the buyer said, "Why, I had a customer in here when we opened it up, and we sold it even before it came out of the box. Send us more just like it!"

—Elizabeth Butler-Witter
Delray Beach, Florida

I could have told those Northern jewelry buyers a thing or two about Southern women. Restraint is great when it comes to cheesecake and cocktails, but not when it comes to showing off our beauty. When it comes to Pearl Girls and jewelry, you can never have too much of a good thing!

Men Are Optional,
Pearls Are Not

When you get ready to entertain, put on your pearls and your party face! Whatever look you choose, a real Pearl Girl will always dress it up and let it shine. A Pearl Girl knows that high heels are appropriate for any occasion (no matter what her mother-in-law says). A lot of things are optional at a party, but pearls (natural, cultured, or just plain fake) are not. Remember, being a beautiful hostess is about attitude, and jewelry is always necessary for a Southern jewel.

Goodness Gracious!

We Southern girls aren't the first belles to love pearls. Cleopatra was reported to have swallowed pearls as a symbol of her endless extravagance, and Elizabeth I of England is said to have worn pearls in abundance to symbolize her virginity.

SOUTHERN TRANSLATION

tee-totaler [tē tōt´ l ər] n. *A Pearl Girl who leaves the house wearing her T-shirt without pearls. It better be an emergency (and even that excuse is suspect)!*

We Southern ladies love diamonds, rubies, and emeralds, but pearls are our birthright. If you want to shine as a hostess, there's never an occasion or time of day when pearls are inappropriate. Several dramatic strands or a choker are great at night, and a single strand is wonderful in the daytime. Just throw on some pearls (and to highlight those pearls, a pearly white smile), and you're ready to take on even the most grueling crowd.

The Hostess with the Mostess, and Other Southern Ladies (and Gentlemen) We Love

Even in the land of Pearl Girls, a few hostesses have shone above others. These are just a few of the Southern ladies (and gentlemen) we can love and learn from.

Helen Keller

No one could have guessed that seven-year-old Helen Keller—deaf and blind since she was nineteen months old, would go on to become one of the most famous women in the world. With the help of her remarkable teacher, Anne Sullivan, Helen Keller was given the gift of language.

A true Southern lady with a generous heart, Helen did not keep her gifts to herself. She traveled throughout the world, bringing hope to the blind and the deaf. Helen was gifted intellectually—she was well known in her lifetime as a writer—but she also had a gift with people. Helen included among her friends presidents, artists, and inventors.

Helen was not just an advocate for the blind and deaf and an author—she was a hostess, as well. Her home became a stopping place for her friends, both famous and ordinary, and her kindness, generosity, and quick mind made her sought out even as she neared the end of her life. Though she died in 1968, Helen Keller still plays the Southern hostess. Each June, thousands of visitors come to Tuscumbia, Alabama, for a weeklong festival honoring the town's most famous daughter.

Dolley Madison

"Delightful Dolley" was the wife of James Madison and a model Southern hostess. She was born in North  Carolina and moved to Virginia (and, of course, Washington, D.C.). She's been called the "first lady of America," some say originating what we still call presidential wives today. She was always a lady, but her idea of elegance was more American than European. She pampered her guests. To her, "abundance was preferable to elegance." Europeans might have scoffed at this idea, but her guests never complained—in fact, they loved her.

Her food was legendary. Dolley Madison introduced ice

cream to the White House, and I'm sure glad she did, because it helped to popularize that wonderful treat for the rest of us. A popular snack cake company is named after her. I grew up eating those delicious Dolley Madison cakes—if I weren't watching my figure, I'd be munching on some right now.

Like any good Southern hostess, Mrs. Madison valued people more than anything. She presided over the first presidential ball and was the first to decorate the president's mansion. She held legendary Wednesday-night receptions. A couple of her traditions still survive today, such as the annual Easter egg roll. No matter what she did, though, it was her personality that people remembered, probably because she made her guests feel special. She cared so much for people, in fact, that when President Madison died, she personally answered every condolence letter.

Pearl Mesta

Although Pearl Reid Skirvin Mesta was born in Michigan, she grew up in Oklahoma, so we can claim this Pearl as one of our own. Ms. Mesta threw such lavish political and social parties in Washington, D.C., that in honor of her efforts, she was appointed "envoy extraordinary and minister plenipotentiary to Luxembourg" by President Truman. She didn't just entertain the elite—Pearl also cared about ordinary servicemen. In fact, she supposedly entertained more than twenty-five thousand men in uniform during World War II. She was so well known, in fact, that a Broadway musical was created loosely based on her life, including the song "Hostess with the Mostess!"

Mary Randolph was born on a Virginia plantation to an elite family. (She was related to Thomas Jefferson.) Like many women of her class and time, she was brought up to be the mistress of a large home, and among her talents was cooking. After her family suffered some economic setbacks, Mary opened a boardinghouse to help support her family. At the boardinghouse, she honed her skills in the kitchen, and her table became well known throughout Virginia.

After retiring from the boardinghouse business, Mary decided to share her knowledge with other women, and she wrote *The Virginia Housewife*. This book was hugely popular and went through several printings throughout the nineteenth century. Women loved her practical approach, which could really be used in an American kitchen. Her commonsense advice rang true for American women: "Let everything be done at the proper time, keep everything in the proper place, and put everything to its proper use." Her advice is still good today. (I'd be a better cook if I could follow it—where'd I put that colander again?) Indeed, she teaches her readers to make the kind of food you might see on a Southern table today: glazed ham, macaroni and cheese, turnips and bacon, corn bread, and sweet potato pudding.

Truman Capote

Leave it to a Southern boy (born in New Orleans and raised in Alabama) to throw the ultimate New York party! His Black and White Ball was considered by many to be the biggest society party of the 1960s. He may not be a Pearl Girl, but he shows that Southern entertaining is famous above the Mason-Dixon line!

Debutante Parties—The Only Place Where a Lady Can Wear White and Have Two Escorts

The debutante ball was once the time when a blushing young belle, dressed in pure white, was presented before the rest of polite society. In the modern South, of course, our daughters don't spend their youths holed up in some boarding school or nursery—they're out there playing soccer and going to college and working in offices. Here in the South, we still put women on a pedestal, and the tradition of the debutante ball continues.

A PEARL GIRL KNOWS

Gentlemen know what makes a Southern belle ring—diamonds, emeralds, rubies, sapphires, and, of course, pearls. And Southern ladies know that it doesn't take a gentleman for them to sparkle. If you've got the money, sugar, there's nothing wrong with buying a little something to make yourself shine like the star you are.

The debutante ball is the culmination of a series of parties welcoming a young woman into society (and into the gaze of young men). The tradition began up North in 1798, when Philadelphia's leading families held a dance assembly for their daughters. Since then, we in the South have made the tradition our own, and each debutante ball is surrounded by its own special rites and traditions, with just a few common rules: The young woman will wear white, she will carry a small bouquet of flowers, and she will receive her guests alongside the hostess.

Goodness Gracious!

At North Carolina's prestigious Terpsichorea Club, sheets were laid out under the debutantes so that their dresses would not be stained. The young women had personalized stools to lift them off the ground and keep their petticoats in place.

Traditionally, debutante balls are only for girls born with silver spoons in their mouths (and lots of silver in their pocketbooks!). But there's no reason that you can't let your daughters "come out" on their own. Dress up a home, or rent a location, and invite your daughter's young friends for an afternoon tea or a dance. Shopping malls are increasingly available for rental, and most young people would think it was fun to have a "mall ball." They can wear white, bring their favorite escort (or just their daddies), and know that they have entered the most elite society of all—that of your friends and family.

Debutante balls seem to attract strange names like molasses draws the flies. A few of the stranger ones:

Montgomery, Alabama
Mardi Gras Ball of the Male Crewe of the Phantom Host and Female Mystic Order of Minerva
(*Whew, try saying that one fast five times!*)

Mobile, Alabama
Beginning of Americas Mystic Society (Leading debutante is the Queen of Mardi Gras with King Felix III from Athelston Club.)

New Orleans, Louisiana
Les Débuts des Jeunes Filles de la Nouvelle Orléans

Richmond, Virginia
Baldreu Bots, June at C.C. of Virginia

Raleigh, North Carolina
Terpsichorean Club

Birmingham, Alabama
Red Stone Club Christmas Ball

Charleston, South Carolina
Daughters of the SOB (South of Broad Street)

CHAPTER 3

The Good Guest

I believe that in the South, even though everything is on the fast track now, there is still more time taken to stop and acknowledge who we're living with and to acknowledge the traditions and rituals of everyday existence.

—DIXIE CARTER
MCLEMORESVILLE, TENNESSEE (PLUS A
LITTLE HOLLYWOOD AND NEW YORK)

Manners maketh man.
—WILLIAM OF WYKEHAM
(SINCE HE DIED IN THE FIFTEENTH
CENTURY, WE CAN'T BLAME HIM FOR
NOT BEING RAISED IN THE SOUTH!)

I F YOU'VE BEEN INVITED TO A REAL SOUTHERN PARTY, ANY-
thing from a hoedown to a housewarming, there's more to
being a good guest than showing up at the door with a bag
of chips and a six-pack of beer. Pearl Girls know that being a
good guest is more than being a warm body. Being a good
guest starts before you even walk in the door, and it ends
with genuine thanks. We Pearl Girls get invited back again
and again, and it isn't just because of our fabulous hair.

Remember Your Upbringing

Always remember your upbringing, unless, of course, you
were brought up in a barnyard or (I don't fault you, sugar) by
Yankees. It starts from the minute you receive an invitation.
Always RSVP. Now, we know that some of those invitations
will say "Regrets Only," and of course you should send polite
regrets if you can't come, but Pearls Girls respond to each
and every invitation. Letting your host or hostess know you
can attend lets them know that you value their invitation,
and that you're looking forward to spending time with them.
And, goodness knows, Pearl Girls want any excuse they can
to talk with their friends and family.

Goodness Gracious!

RSVP is the abbreviation of the French phrase, "répondez s'il vous plaît." No matter how often Cousin Ronny says otherwise, it does not mean "respond soon, very promptly" or even "Ronny's swinging voodoo party."

The hosts of large events often enclose a self-addressed stamped envelope and reply card with their invitations. Now, these make matters much easier for the host, especially if she's sending out several hundred invitations, but they don't leave much room for Pearl Girls to let their personalities shine. By all means, send back that card, but it is also nice to enclose a personal note.

If you've been invited to a less formal event, you probably won't receive an RSVP card. If so, the best thing to do is send your own card accepting or regretting. Remember all those hours your grammar school teacher made you sit copying your letters? Well, now is the time for that work to pay off. A handwritten note shows your hostess that you care, and it's a great excuse to use that beautiful stationery you've been saving up.

For a very informal event (a night drinking margaritas with the girls and laughing at your husbands—and that *is* what we're talking about, boys) a friendly phone call is all that's necessary.

Once you've accepted in a way that'd make your mama proud, don't embarrass her by forgetting the date. Write it down, stick it on your fridge, or get a tattoo—whatever it takes to remember your obligation. When the date and time come, show up, and show up on time. For a cocktail party or another event that isn't seated, it is standard to show up a bit after the official starting hour. (But not a few hours later—showing up at midnight after pounding back tequila shots all evening might make you funnier, but it won't make you more welcome.) For a seated event or for any event featuring a meal, show up at the stated time. Don't let the main course get cold because you needed an extra hour to highlight your hair. We Pearl Girls are special enough so that people will wait for us, but we don't force them to do it.

A PEARL GIRL KNOWS

Never accept an invitation from someone you wouldn't want to have back at your own house.

Always show up in the proper dress. For a formal evening event, if the invitation does not say "black tie optional" or something else indicating casual dress, the assumption is that the evening is black tie. Now, I know we Pearl Girls love playing dress up, even when we're eighty, so we girls are not only willing to show up in our dresses and heels, we'll be waiting for the chance to do so. It might be a bit more trouble getting the man in your life to put on a monkey suit. If it helps, bribe him with promises of his favorite dessert or kisses. (Kisses from us Pearl Girls are sweeter than honey anyway, and won't give him a potbelly.) If all else fails, buy NASCAR tickets, and tell him you'll go without him if he doesn't dress right.

For less formal events, it's sometimes hard to tell how you should dress. For evening events that are more casual, a nicer dress or pantsuit is always appropriate. For daytime events, a sundress or a skirt and blouse are usually correct.

Tuxedos Aren't Just
for Penguins

Like any good Southern girl, I love to dress up for a High-Falutin' affair. My dear ex-husband (Bless His Heart #3), on the other hand, was another story. During the early nineties, we planned to attend the Zoobilee, a black tie evening to benefit the Birmingham Zoo. I shopped for weeks, had my nails done, and styled my hair just so. My husband, on the other hand, was a little (well, a lot) tight with his money. I started asking him to rent a tuxedo months in advance, and he hemmed and hawed. A couple of weeks before the event, I laid down the law, and he finally admitted that he had no plans to rent anything—his plain old suit was going to have to be good enough. Tuxedos, he thought, were optional, and insisted that his dark suit would be just fine for a black tie evening.

On the night of the big event, I looked like a movie star, and he looked like an undertaker. I don't have to tell a good Southern girl what it was like to be turned away at the door because he was dressed inappropriately! Usually, a "bless his heart" is enough when men act like men, but this time he got an earful! In fact, the next year, I left him at home with a TV dinner and attended the party myself!

—Deborah Ford
  Birmingham, Alabama

(Just wear what you'd wear to church.) For tailgating or sports, slacks and a shirt are usually appropriate (but no UNC gear at a Duke fan's party, even if you think Coach K is starting to sprout tiny little horns). If you have no idea, feel free to call up your hostess and ask her what she's planning to wear. Follow her lead, and you'll always be in the proper attire. But don't follow too close—and for heaven's sake, don't try to outblonde her!

A PEARL GIRL KNOWS

One rule of thumb to follow (aside from not wearing white after Labor Day, but that's not something I need to tell Pearl Girls) is that the earlier the party starts, the more conservative the dress. That sequined gold lamé halter top may show off your tan perfectly, but it would be out of place at a bridal luncheon.

For most parties, it is appropriate to bring an escort, and the invitation will usually indicate that you should do so. If the invitation does not say so, it is perfectly fine to ask if you can bring a date, but be prepared for your hostess to say no, especially at something like a seated business function. Unless the invitation specifies otherwise, it is not appropriate to bring your next-door neighbor, college buddy, Uncle Herman, and the guy who pumps your gas (unless he's your date, of course). A polite invitation will not tell you to leave your kids at home, but a Pearl Girl knows that children are not invited unless asked. The exception is a family event, such as a wedding (or Vernon's Memorial Day Bud-in-the-Bird-Cook-a-Thon), where you are expected to bring your whole family.

If you have houseguests, a polite host may ask you to bring them along. You may call the hostess and say, "We're having some old college friends that weekend, and we'd hate to leave them at home." She'll either accept your regrets, or (the Pearl Girls way) ask them to come along. Whatever you do, though, don't just show up to a party with a contingent of your husband's old frat buddies. They might have fun playing drinking games on your hostess's antique coffee table, but you won't be invited back again.

A good hostess won't turn you away if you show up in nothing but your clothes and a smile (and at some parties—not the ones a Pearl Girl like me attends—just the smile is enough), but your presence will be even more welcome when you have a hostess gift. For some parties—weddings, baby or bridal showers, housewarmings—a gift is mandatory. For others—dinner parties, cocktail parties, bridge luncheons—it is just a courtesy.

If you do bring a gift, try to put yourself in the hostess's shoes. A bunch of flowers is pretty, but you'll send your hostess scurrying around for a nice vase when she should be attending to guests. For a dinner party or another party with a set menu (as opposed to a pot luck or an informal buffet), a cooked dish or dessert will interfere with what your hostess planned for supper. Better choices are gifts that let the hostess know you care but that she won't have to use right away—wine or liquor, chocolates, potpourri, candles, or soap. Wine and liquor are excellent choices for a cocktail party, especially if your hosts are younger people (or young at heart). Just leave that half-finished bottle of white lightning at home—nothing is tackier than bringing your leftovers to a party.

A Southern Spouse in the Service

When I said "I do" to my best friend and the man of my dreams, I soon learned the mantra "Home is where the air force sends us." Being married to Douglas, I got used to being carted all over the country. Then the day came when my entire life changed. The phone rang, and when I answered my husband's voice was on the other end. "Dear, I have news," he said, waiting for me to respond. I could tell it was something big, something he was afraid to say. I tried to stay calm and asked what his news was. His next sentence would put me in shock. "I got orders today. We're going to Germany." Of course I didn't believe him until he walked in the door with the papers in his hand. I was shocked and scared, but when things go "south," I remember what my mother told me every time I faced a challenge. She said, "You are your mama's child." I didn't understand what she meant until now: I am the daughter of a strong Southern woman, and I can do anything!

Southern food (good old chocolate gravy isn't something you can find in the land of brochen and bratwurst) and Southern hospitality are what I miss most about the States. My husband's coworkers are still impressed when I send a dish to work with him. Recently, he had a party at work, and I sent a cake, truffles, and chocolate candy. They thought I went out of my way, but I explained that cooking is a Southern thing—it's my comfort! To a Southern girl, going out of your way is part of being a good guest, and it's a part of the South that I can carry with me wherever I go. I'm looking forward to our next posting, wherever that may be, and showing our foreign friends why we Southern girls are welcomed wherever we go.

—Donna Porter
Germany (at least until the air force moves us!)

A PEARL GIRL KNOWS

If your hostess is pregnant, nursing, or a Baptist, a bottle of nonalcoholic cider or grape juice is a thoughtful way to let her sip a cocktail at her own party.

A short cocktail party really requires nothing from you but some interesting conversation and the proper thanks, though of course gifts are appreciated. If you're a houseguest, however, a gift is mandatory. For longer stays, you can offer to prepare a meal for your hosts and the other guests, though be prepared for your hostess to reject the offer—we Pearl Girls like to pamper our guests ourselves. If you are cooking, bring along your own food and any special cooking equipment, and give the kitchen a thorough cleaning when you're done, or, better yet, get an available male to do the cleaning for you. A food gift, especially breakfast foods or sweets that can be served in addition to whatever the hostess has planned, will be appreciated. (An overnight stay is not like a dinner party, where adding a course of your own food might inconvenience the host.) Anything for the home is appreciated, especially if you're at a second home (hunting cabin, beach house, ski condo), which may not be as well stocked as a primary residence. If you do give something for the home, give it graciously. Don't hand over new bath towels and say, "I noticed you had ratty and stained old towels that a highway motel would throw away." Say, "I always like having extra towels around, so I thought you would, too."

For an overnight stay, a quick bread makes a nice gift. Your hostess can serve it for breakfast, lay it out for an afternoon snack, or keep it for herself.

Pumpkin Bread

1 ⅓ cups sifted flour
1 teaspoon baking soda
¾ teaspoon salt
1 ½ teaspoons cinnamon
Generous grating of fresh nutmeg (or 1/4 teaspoon preground)
½ teaspoon dry ginger
1 ½ cups sugar
2 large eggs
⅓ cup water
1 cup canned pumpkin
½ cup neutral oil, such as canola

Preheat oven to 350 degrees F. In a large mixing bowl, combine the dry ingredients. In a separate bowl, stir together wet ingredients, then add to the dry, stirring until the batter is just combined. (Don't overstir or you'll get a tough batter filled with air bubbles.) Pour the batter into a greased, floured loaf pan. Bake for 1 hour or until top is firm to the touch. Allow the bread to cool. You may add a large handful of chopped pecans or other nuts, raisins, dried cranberries, or chocolate chips to the batter before baking for variety. Don't add all of them, though, or the bread will fall apart. (And then you'll have to eat the whole thing yourself, and your waistline won't thank you for that!)

When in the South, Do as Your Hostess Does

You may not know a soup tureen from a ramekin, but it doesn't matter. Follow your hostess's lead, and you won't go wrong. At a small, formal dinner, watch your hostess, and don't start eating until she does. If you're seated at separate tables, wait until everyone at your table is served; then dig in. At a less formal dinner, don't pick off the buffet until the hostess ushers the guests in (preferably in small groups). At a cocktail party, those nibbles are out for the taking, so if you want one of those crazy little hot dogs, go ahead and grab one before the linebacker takes them all.

Goodness Gracious!

There was a time when a hostess would speak to the guest on her right at the beginning of the meal. The guests would follow her lead. Then, halfway through the meal, she'd start speaking to the person on her left, and the other guests would follow her. This custom, called "turning the table," no longer exists, but a polite hostess (and a polite guest), should make time for the persons on both her right and left.

The best rule for dealing with any uncertain situation, from eating an artichoke to cleaning your fingers, is to watch what your hostess does. Does she put the tough little leaves she's finished back on her plate or into a waiting bowl? Doing what she does avoids the sticky situation of putting your shrimp shells into a bread basket. She may not always be "right" in the way an etiquette book teaches—she may leave her finger bowl on her plate rather than placing it, doily and all, to the upper left of her place setting—just pay her no mind. It's her party, honey.

SOUTHERN TRANSLATION

finger bowl [fin´ gər bōl] **n.** *a small bowl filled with water, and perhaps a slice of lemon, served at or near the end of a meal. The guests dip the fingers of each hand in the bowl, then blot dry on their napkins. Not to be used as a mouthwash (though believe it or not, that used to be standard practice!) and never use to serve fingers. President Martin Van Buren allegedly rolled up his sleeves and washed his entire arms in the bowl—not the Pearl Girl way, but, bless him, even the president of the United States is a man in need of female guidance sometimes.*

The Right Table and the Right Seat

At a formal dinner, finding the right table and the right seat is easy—just sit where the place card tells you, even if it means rubbing elbows with a man whose idea of polite dinner conversation is talking about his colonoscopy. Your hostess will have thought out her seating plan well in advance, and trading place cards, or simply sitting at someone else's seat, will interfere. You'll have to hear the gory details for a couple hours at maximum, so put on your best Pearl Girl smile and suffer through it. (Who knows, you might even learn something.)

At a larger formal dinner, where there are multiple tables, a seating chart should be provided at the entrance to the room (often in a leather binder, if you have trouble finding it). If there is no seating chart, don't call it to the attention of the hostess. Simply look for the right table and sit on down. It isn't the Pearl Girl way to call our hostess's attention to an oversight.

A PEARL GIRL KNOWS

If conversation flags, there are two topics we Pearl Girls could talk about for hours: "How's your motha?" and "I love your haira!"

If you're a woman, feel free to sit down when you enter the dining room. The hostess should be the last to sit, but don't worry if she sits first. Men should not be seated until all the women are seated, and they should draw out the chair for the woman to their right. Since sometimes our men need a bit of gentle training (it's hard enough for them to remember to use a fork and to wipe their hands on a napkin, not a tie), a quick reminder before entering the dining room will help everyone. To help the man next to you pull out your chair, it's easiest if you stand to the right of your seat. If he forgets, pull it out yourself, smile, and remember that not all men can be proper Southern gentlemen (and don't bless his heart . . . bless his mama's).

A PEARL GIRL KNOWS

If you sit down at a formal table and find that it is set incorrectly, leave everything where it is. It may be poor form to set your table incorrectly, but it is even worse to call everyone's attention to the error. Pearl Girls know that the secret to etiquette is not knowing where to put the shrimp fork—it's making those around us comfortable and happy.

At less formal dinners, guests will often seat themselves. As much as we love the company of our male escorts, or our best friends, we Pearl Girls should share ourselves with people we don't know. Sit separately from your escort, and try to make conversation with someone you don't know. Guests will often try to sit male-female, but if that isn't possible, don't worry. Go ahead and sit next to a woman you don't know that well, and get yourself a new girlfriend!

What Do I Do With . . . ?

Cocktail glass. Leave it in the room where you had your before-dinner drinks. Don't take it to the table. You'll interfere with the hostess's table setting and, besides, that fuzzy navel or Long Island iced tea probably doesn't complement the vichyssoise.

Handbag. If you're in a private home, leave it where the hostess indicates. She'll usually have a spare bedroom reserved for coats and bags. When we're in the homes of Pearl Girls, we don't have to worry about the safety of our things.

If you're in a restaurant, banquet hall, or club, keep it in your lap or on the floor by your feet. Hanging your bag on the back of your chair may interfere with your servers (especially if you have a small bathroom cabinet of cosmetics in there), and it is an invitation to prying hands.

Napkin. When you need to leave the table, leave your napkin on your seat. At the end of the meal, loosely fold it and lay it on the table, or, if there's a napkin ring, place the napkin loosely through the ring. Whatever you do, don't use the napkin as a handkerchief. Tending to your nose is something a lady never does at the table.

Toothpick. If the hostess has left little receptacles, such as ashtrays, around the room, leave them there. If not, place it in a wastebasket. It isn't proper to leave a toothpick on the serving tray, on a houseplant, in your teeth, or tucked into your hairdo. (God forbid!)

Teaspoon. When drinking iced tea, leave the spoon in the glass. Hold it out of the way with a finger while you sip. For hot tea, place the spoon on your saucer, not on the tablecloth.

Goodness Gracious!

In the nineteenth century, it was considered proper to pour hot tea into a saucer, wait for it to cool, and then sip it straight from the saucer. Don't let your mama see you do this today!

Retainer. This advice is mainly for teenaged children, though some of us (me included) had braces as adults. Remove your retainer discreetly, behind a napkin if you need to do so at the table, but better yet in the restroom. Keep the retainer in its case, not wrapped in a napkin. (Not only is wrapping it and leaving it in a napkin unappetizing, but digging through the laundry or, worse, the garbage later is downright disgusting.)

Husband. Leave him be and hope he doesn't tell that story about catching that giant bass again.

Ten Rules to Get through a Lead Crystal and Candlelight Affair

You're at a formal dinner, and your idea of classy food is unwrapping the burgers ahead of time. How do you cope? Well, if you're a Southern girl, it's no problem. You keep a smile on your face and follow a few simple rules, and people will be thinking you've been jetting off to the Riviera all your life.

1. If you're confronted with an array of flatware, some of which looks as if it might be used in complex dental surgery, don't panic. Generally, you start at the outside of your place setting and work your way in. So the fork for the earliest course will be on your far right, and the fork for the main course will be closest to the plate. When in doubt, just look what your hostess is doing. If you're still in doubt, just grab whatever fork

is handy and dig in—as long as you're polite and confident, no one cares that you just ate the avocado with a crab fork.

2. Your knife is not for scratching your back, gutting a fish, or picking your teeth. It's for carefully cutting your food into small portions. When you aren't using it, keep it in your hand or on the edge of your plate, not on the tablecloth. A lot of people, especially in bigger cities, eat Continental style, meaning the knife stays in the right hand and the fork in the left, throughout the meal. You may look like a cheese-eating surrender monkey, but you avoid any awkward moments of trying to figure out where to rest your silverware.

3. Talk to your neighbors. You may have a billionaire, research scientist, hot male stripper who volunteers with children on your right and Uncle Ernie on your left, but try to give them both equal time. And who knows, maybe Uncle Ernie has discovered the secret to losing weight on a diet of tequila and chocolate. You'll never know until you talk to him.

4. If you don't like something, pretend you don't notice. You may think that the only place sushi belongs is on the end of a fishing pole, but a dinner party is not the time to let those feelings out. If something isn't prepared well, "I'm getting full" is better than "This smells worse than my husband's jogging shorts." If your flatware or glass is not clean, and you're at a restaurant or banquet hall, feel free to ask for another, but in a private home, it's better to say nothing.

5. Unless the hostess breaks out the forty-ounce tall boys after dinner and challenges you to a game of quarters, a formal dinner is not the time to show how much alcohol you can handle. Many formal dinners will have a substantial amount of alcohol served—predinner drinks, a wine with most courses, and a liqueur after coffee. Know your limits, and know that a polite signal will stop your hosts from pouring. After all, do you want to be the person who sang "I Did It My Way" on the coffee table while doing a striptease? Well, maybe you do, put probably not at a formal dinner.

6. Unless they were invited explicitly, leave the kids with Grandma or a sitter. Especially if all they'll eat is peanut butter and the hosts are serving rack of lamb with zinfandel sauce.

7. At a formal dinner, the food is often presented to each guest for serving. Take the serving fork in your left hand, the spoon in your right, and serve yourself. Try to take a modest portion. I know that you would never let your guests go hungry—Southern girls love to feed people—but your host may have underestimated, and you don't want anyone to go without.

8. Unless you're under six years old, you don't need a bib. On a visit to New York City, each and every one of my companions tucked his napkin behind his tie. Now, these boys were Yankees and can't be expected to know better, but Southern ladies and gentlemen know that when we're eating something messy, we carefully lean over the bowl or plate, and hold the napkin up if we feel it's necessary. We don't tuck our napkins into our shirts like a frat boy at an all-u-can-eat barbecue.

9. Write a thank-you note. Even if the roast was burnt, the hostess was drunk, and you suffered a bad case of food poisoning.

10. Don't worry. There's no mistake you can make that hasn't been made before. Enjoy yourself and your neighbors, and have fun. It's a party, not an algebra quiz. So show them just how fun it is to be Southern!

You Want Me to Eat That? How to Handle Everything from Artichokes to Zinfandel

As always, the rule is that if you do not know, watch your hostess. If you're the host, don't ever serve anything that you aren't absolutely sure how to eat. Remember that every eye is on you!

Artichokes. There's a story that during World War II, the French took revenge on their German "guests" by serving them artichokes. Believe it or not, though, that overgrown green pinecone is not only edible but delicious to boot! Pull off each leaf individually, dip it in whatever sauce is provided, and then scrape off the pulp with your teeth. Discard the remainder of the leaf (on your plate or a dish provided, not over your shoulder). When you reach the soft inner part of the artichoke, use your knife and fork.

Asparagus. Etiquette books will tell you that stalks may be eaten with the fingers. While this may be technically correct, it's messy, and people who don't know better will think you were raised in a barn. Use a knife and fork, and you'll always look like a lady. The exception is when the asparagus is cut in short stalks and served as part of a crudité platter. Since you'd look strange cutting up the finger food with a knife and fork, go ahead and dig in.

Chicken or Chops. At any kind of formal event, use a knife and fork. Fried chicken is usually served at informal events only, and may be eaten with the hands. At an informal event, it's fine to pick up the bones to get every delicious bit, but, heavens, don't grab the bone off someone else's plate. (And advise your man that that behavior is best left at home along with his favorite baseball cap.)

Corn. We could fill pages with debates over how to eat corn on the cob. I say any way is fine as long as you have fun! Just wipe those pretty fingers (and lips and cheeks) when you're done!

Fish. Occasionally a hostess will serve a whole fish, head and all. "It's staring at me," is not the proper response. Eating a whole fish is surprisingly easy once you get the hang of it. Separate the head from the body, slit the body open (if it isn't slit already), lay the fish open flat on your plate, then lift out the skeleton (using the fish knife to loosen it from the body). A fish knife is not really for cutting—it's for the process just described and separating the meat of the fish into large flakes.

Lobster. Along with whole fish, lobsters are a time-honored manner of torturing guests at formal meals. Fortunately, they're delicious, so once you get the hang of it, you'll look forward to seeing that red body glaring up at you from the plate. Begin by taking the large claws from the body with a twist and pull. Remove the shell with crackers, and pull out the meat with a small fork. (A thoughtful hostess will pre-crack the shell, making this process much easier.) Twist off the little claws, and suck out the meat. (If you think these little things are more trouble than they're worth, leave them alone.) Break off the little flippers from the end of the tail, split the tail, then remove the tail and eat with a knife and fork. Some people eat the green liver and the roe from the body, but if you're new to this, I suggest that you leave it to the experts.

Olives. If olives are served with the pit, eat the olive, then delicately remove the pit from your mouth (cover with a napkin while you do this), and discard.

Oysters. Raw oysters can be eaten by picking up the oyster by the shell and picking it out with your fork, but some folks think it's a lot more fun to pick up the shell and slurp the whole thing out. Personally, I find this uncouth. Cooked oysters, on the other hand, are always eaten with the utensils provided.

Zinfandel. Wineglasses should always be held by the stem rather than the bowl. Doing so keeps the wine from heating up (including red wine, which is not chilled, but isn't heated up by hot little hands either). Before drinking, blot your lipstick so that you won't end up with more makeup on the glass than on your face.

We Pearl Girls know that the best way to get through any social situation isn't sparkling wit or sparkling earrings, it's manners, manners, manners. From the time we're the smallest little Pearl Girls, our mamas taught us to treat our elders with respect, to apologize and say thank you, and to share our chocolate bars. Once we're adults, we don't forget those manners. To Pearl Girls, manners aren't about knowing a load of fancy rules of etiquette. Manners are about putting those around you at ease. If we're in doubt about our behavior, we Pearl Girls ask ourselves one simple question: Is what I'm doing going to make me a more pleasant person to be around? If the answer is yes, we smile and let our Pearl Girls personality shine. Pretty is as pretty does, and we Pearl Girls always want to be gorgeous—inside and out.

Goodness Gracious!

In the Colonial United States, beverages in taverns were served in pint and quart containers. When a guest would be a little rowdy, the tavern keeper would shout "mind your p's and q's" to keep him in line. When we tell our rowdy little sons and daughters today to mind their p's and q's, let's hope it's sugar hepping them up, and not ale.

Remember how your mama always taught you to say "you first"? Well, that rule still applies when you're an adult. Go ahead and let the other person step in front of you at the

Who Are Your People?

When we Pearl Girls are having trouble making conversation with a stranger, we know one tried and true way to get things started. Catherine P. McLean is a Pearl Girl through and through. Born in Double Springs, Alabama, in 1930, she's lived in Auburn, Tuscaloosa, Talladega, Huntsville, and was "raised in a Topsy-Turnover combination in North Carolina, Florida, and Alabama during the WWII years." She's a woman who had the Pearl Girls " 'tude way 'fore it was so titled."

When Mrs. McLean is having trouble making conversation, she knows that one surefire way to get started is asking about family. She mentions "Davison, Loard, McCrary, Hays, Wood, Wingard, Reich, Nalty, Nesmith . . . just to name a few." And if that doesn't find some relation, she keeps digging. We Pearl Girls figure that we all go back to Adam, so if we dig far enough, we can find some relation.

buffet or the bar. It gives you an extra minute to make up your mind between the ham and the turkey anyway.

And if your mother was anything like mine, she taught you never to leave anyone out. That means going up to the stranger and introducing yourself, and trying to make sure that no one sits by themselves in a corner. Your hostess will thank you for making her job easier, and you'll get to meet someone new. Besides, we Pearl Girls don't want to be self-ish—we should share ourselves with everyone!

When you do make conversation with that stranger, keep religion and politics out of your small talk. A Southern Baptist and an atheist can get along like a pig and mud, but only if they leave their religious beliefs at the door. Differences between family members and close friends can be lively, but they shouldn't get out of hand because you have love holding you together. When you've got nothing in common but your hostess and the cocktail weenies, leave sensitive subjects out of the conversation. Besides, wouldn't you rather talk about a trip to the Bahamas than predestination?

A PEARL GIRL KNOWS

Although Pearl Girls know that sterling silver is usually stamped STERLING *or* 925 *on the back, we'd never get caught looking!*

And leave that dirty linen back home where it belongs! Your mother-in-law may be a certifiable, wicked, devious, two-faced, manipulative nutjob, but that's a matter between the two of you. In public, as my mother used to say (and I'm sure yours did, too), if you don't have something nice to say, don't say anything at all.

Three Days?
Fish and Guests Usually Stink after Three Hours

One of the reasons that we Pearl Girls are welcome wherever we go is that we know when to clear out. Your hostess loves to spend time with you, and she went out of her way to make you happy and comfortable, but the time comes when enough is enough and she just wants to get some beauty sleep.

Aunt Franny's Toast

George and Libby, both in their nineties, are a Southern couple to the bone. Libby would never dream of serving a meal without the correct silverware, and George always leads the family in saying grace. They've brought up three generations of Southern ladies and gentlemen, and they've taught each generation that family matters above all else. I'm proud to be the wife of their grandson and the mother of their great-granddaughter.

Libby is always a proper lady—I've never seen her without her stockings on or her hair done—and I can't imagine anything improper ever crossing her lips. Her sister Franny is also a Southern lady, but of a different sort. Even though she's in her eighties, Franny could beat me hands-down in a dance contest, and she brings laughter with her wherever she goes. If there's a party, Franny's there, and there's no sign of her slowing down any time soon. Aunt Franny loves to talk, and if sometimes something inappropriate slips out, well, that's all the more reason to laugh right along with her.

For their sixtieth wedding anniversary, the whole family gathered at their Louisville, Kentucky, home to thank them for their love and their guidance through the years. We were all gathered on the back porch of the family home, and we had finished a meal served on Libby's best china and linens (impeccably pressed, naturally). The family members began to rise and make their toasts. Aunt Renee presented a scrapbook honoring the family through the years, and those old pictures brought tears to nearly every eye. Their granddaughter Amy and my husband, Bret, presented a picture of the two great-grandbabies. Everyone thought of the happiness and love, even through the hard times, that the family had shared through the years.

Then Aunt Franny stood up. She presented a lovely little plant filled with bright yellow flowers, and she said that we could plant it in the yard and watch it grow through the years. That plant was in honor of something wonderful, something truly great and memorable. She paused for a minute to wipe a stray tear from the corner of her eyes. We all thought that Aunt Franny was thinking about the years that she'd shared with her sister and brother-in-law, until she spoke, that is. She told us that she was presenting the plant in honor of . . . Uncle Stan and his son Garth, who had been kind enough to clean her gutters.

Aunt Franny sat down, and everyone on the porch was silent for a moment. Then the family began to clap, and I have to admit that the younger generation exchanged a few big smiles. Part of being family is loving everyone, even when they make a toast at a wedding anniversary in honor of home maintenance. We'll all be able to share this memory, and I hope someday Bret and I will talk about it on our sixtieth anniversary with our own children gathered around us. That toast made our time just a little bit more memorable and special, just not in a way we expected. You have to love Aunt Franny.

—Elizabeth Butler-Witter
Delray Beach, Florida

At an early cocktail party (something that starts around six or seven), you'll be expected to make your exit pretty quickly. Since the food served is usually light, and a couple of canapés don't sit so well with nothing but a cosmopolitan, most guests will want to get out of there anyway to get something to eat. For an after-dinner cocktail party, guests can sometimes get a little rowdy. Feel free to stay around as long as the party stays fun, but leave as soon as your hostess starts mentioning the hour. (Even better, try to get some guests to leave with you, and offer to drive home anyone who's had more than their share).

Ever been to a dinner party where you're seated between a man who keeps asking you how many Estonians it takes to screw in a lightbulb and one who fell asleep in his soup? Unfortunately, barring a heart attack or seizure (and don't even think about faking it!) it isn't polite to leave a formal dinner until the coffee is served, and it is better to remain for at least an hour to socialize after dinner. At a less formal, unseated affair, remember that people tend to leave after the first guest

How Long Should I Stay?

At most parties, you should watch the other guests and depart when they begin to leave. If the party is still rocking at 3 a.m. (and the hostess is joining in on the fun), feel free to pound back those shooters with the rest of the guests (though not so many that you lose your good manners—you are a Pearl Girl, after all). This guide gives you approximate times of how long to hang around for most major parties:

Coffee with the ladies	1 hour
Cocktail party	2 hours
Tailgate	When the game begins
Watching the big game	1 hour after the game ends
Dinner	1 hour after dinner ends
Shower	Half an hour after the gifts are unwrapped
Wedding	Any time after the bride and groom depart

departs, so try not to hurt your hostess's feelings by walking off before you've sipped even one julep. If you must go early, make sure that you've thanked your hostess.

It's polite to ask your hostess if she wants some help straightening up, but you have no obligation to do so. Unless she's a close friend or family, a good hostess will probably turn down your offer. If you do offer, though, be prepared for her to say yes, roll up your sleeves, and get that house back into a fit condition for a Southern lady.

A PEARL GIRL KNOWS

Sharing your personality with everyone means that you can sometimes get caught in a conversation you don't want to have—an endless tale of a low-down, cheating wife, the gruesome details of arthroscopic surgery, or anything having to do with tax law. Before you leave for a party, make sure you pack a couple of parachutes. If you don't have any other excuses arranged, "I'm sorry, but I just haven't had a chance to thank our beautiful hostess, and she's free now, do you mind?" is a time-honored way to back out.

Thank-You Notes

If you invite a Pearl Girl to a party, she'll send a thank-you note, even if she's still in the hospital recovering from the bad salmon mousse. Remember to thank your hostess, not the guest of honor. At a baby shower, for instance, thank the mother-in-law who threw the party, not the pregnant woman, and certainly not the baby. Pearl Girls send notes for even the most casual tailgating party or Sunday school picnic. And I declare, a real Pearl Girl will send you a thank-you note for lending her a handkerchief.

Always make sure that you send a thank-you note for any gift. Growing up, I never sent thank-you notes for Christmas presents from adults, and I'm embarrassed to say that I didn't teach my daughters to either. Well, my mother-in-law was taught differently, and she didn't appreciate no thanks from my daughters. The lesson I learned is that everyone, even children, should send thanks for gifts.

A PEARL GIRL KNOWS

If you feel it's time to entertain the party with your exotic dance stylings, it's probably time to pack it up and go. You might have a bit less fun, but you won't be wondering why the neighbors are snickering at you the next day.

Thank-you notes let those around us know how much we appreciate them. A good thank-you note should be hand-written, preferably in handwriting better than a drunken baboon's, and it should be on a decent grade of paper, not notebook paper. You don't have to use the best stationery

A PEARL GIRL KNOWS

Your last impression should be as good as your first. Make sure that the heels of your shoes are in good shape, as they are the last thing they'll see as you walk out the door.

Sticky Situations

- **Saying Grace.** *Saying grace (or not) is the responsibility of your host. If saying grace is important to you and you are close to the host, feel free to offer to say a few words of thanks, but be prepared for a no, either because the host wishes to say a few words or the host does not wish to have a group prayer. If you are in a home where the hosts say grace and you do not, bow your head and be silent.*

- **Giving a Toast.** *If you are asked to give a toast, feel free to say nothing more than "Here's to our wonderful hosts." A few personal words or an anecdote are nice, but keep it short. I was once at a wedding reception where the groom's aunt (who was ninety years old and able to get away with pretty much anything) said loudly after an unusually long toast, "Whew, I thought that would never be over!" Don't let this happen to you!*

- **Drunken or Insulting Guests.** *Since you're a Pearl Girl, you'd never get out of hand or say anything inappropriate (and if you do, you'll remember to apologize). A drunken or insulting guest is the responsibility of your hosts. Feel free to walk away or turn your head from someone you find offensive, or politely point out to your hosts that someone seems to be a bit out of hand. Don't start World War Three—the hangover and embarrassment the next morning are punishment enough.*

- **Your Own Blunders.** *You show up in the wrong clothes, knock over the buffet table, and step on the toy poodle. Apologize and offer to fix the problem if you can, whether it's paying the laundry bill or replacing a wine goblet. Once you've apologized profusely, let it go and let the party proceed. If the host or other guests are still agitated, apologize again and leave.*

Get your children started on thank-you notes early by letting them have a little fun. Get together colored paper, magazines to cut up, and some crayons or markers. Mommy and child can have a fun afternoon making a personalized card, and the recipient will have a thank-you note that's one of a kind. Just remember to put a personal note in the envelope yourself so that the recipient will know who's thanking her!

available, but you should use something that shows that you've taken some care.

The secret to a good thank-you note is including at least one personal detail. If you attended a bridal shower, for in-

Thank-You Notes You Wish You'd Sent

Like many Pearl Girls, I've lost some of the most special people in my life before I had time to really thank them. We Pearl Girls should never miss the opportunity to thank those around us, even for the smallest things. Here's a few thank-you notes I wish I had sent:

- *Thank you for helping me when I was feeling down.*
- *Thank you for finally cleaning out the garage.*
- *Thank you for teaching me algebra, even though I fought you all the way.*
- *Thank you for teaching me to make the best homemade fudge in the world.*
- *Thank you for being the best mother ever—for teaching me to pray, to play, and to love.*

stance, it is better to thank your hostess by saying, "I just loved watching little Miss Emily unwrap those gifts. It made me think of my own days as a bride, and I was tickled pink to see her so happy," than "Thanks for inviting me to the shower." Mentioning one thing that happened at the party not only shows that you're truly grateful, but it also shows that you're not sending a form letter. If you've received a gift from your hostess, write about using the gift. "We ate those delicious caramels together the next day and laughed about Mr. Johnson's jokes" is always better than "Thanks for the candy, girlfriend."

And remember, Pearl Girls know that it's better to thank people too often than not enough.

As a surprise for a very busy attorney friend of mine, Wendy Tunstill, I dropped a present off at her office. For weeks, I heard nothing from her, and I was afraid that she didn't get the gift. I finally called to ask if she had received it.

Now, my friend is a professional woman in her mid-thirties, but her reply was something that Pearl Girls of every age can relate to: "Oh, I'm so sorry," she said. "Please don't call my mother!"

My reply was, "Please don't call my mother for asking!"

—Deborah Ford
Birmingham, Alabama

Give Me that Old Time Religion!

Whether we're foot-washing Baptists or strait-laced Episcopalians, religion is central to who we are as Southerners. Religion for us is not something dour or a boring duty—it is a central part of a life well-lived. Religion is not just Sunday services, weddings, and funerals: it's Wednesday-night prayer meetings, Sunday school parties, creek baptisms, all-day sings, cemetery cleaning, fish fries, revival meetings, covered-dish suppers, youth group picnics, and church bazaars. Religion renews our spirit and opens our hearts. We make a joyful noise before the Lord and celebrate!

Homecoming

Claire walked toward the gate of the church cemetery. Rehoboth Baptist Church, a white clapboard building nestled in a pine grove, had stood in this location for more than 125 years. It was a stable sight in an unstable world. The tall steeple tolled its bell for sinner and saint.

She stopped under the shade of the tall trees that graced the church and thought of the hands that had built the church and planted the trees. She set down her burdens on the sturdy plank tables beneath the trees and began unpacking. She brushed away pine needles and began to spread her favorite tablecloth—a red and white checkered pattern she'd used for years—over the rough planks. She took out a casserole dish (her husband called it her church-lady dish), still warm from the oven. She'd made her almost-famous chicken-and-rice dish (almost famous because last year Jenny had made chicken and wild rice that everyone had raved over—Claire thought wild rice was no better than a weed). The thick, quilted tablecloth would keep the food warm for a while.

Claire was unpacking her cake when Lula Wanamaker came down

the path loudly singing "Bringing in the Sheaves." Lula was the church pianist and could always be heard humming or singing something.

"Claire Walker, how in goodness are you?" Lula said, setting down a dish of her famous deviled eggs.

"How many do you suppose we can count on seeing?" Claire set out a Lane Cake that set her mouth watering. They never knew how many might show up.

"Maybe one hundred. That's a few less than last year—some of the older folks aren't feeling so well anymore."

"What makes them come back, year after year? The same folks, the same weekend, the same place? Do you think we're called back?" Claire wondered.

"Oh, no," Lula laughed. "It's the food. Definitely the food. Where else can you go, eat your favorite foods, pay your respects to folks you've known your whole life, and go home to tell your neighbors you had lunch in a cemetery?"

Lula's laugh carried down the path and welcomed several more ladies bearing boxes and baskets of lovingly prepared food. Boxes were emptied. Strains of joyful voice lifted in a common goal. The preservation of a tradition passed on from mother to daughter. A chance to say thank you to all those who've gone before you.

It was Homecoming Sunday at Rehoboth Baptist Church, and the church ladies were on the job.

—Patti Holladay
   Cartersville, Georgia

CHAPTER 4

The Weeks Before

Deep South parties are a combination of old world elegance and downright Southern vulgarity. . . . Confederate balls and holiday cocktail parties nip in the bud any tendency towards putting on airs, as the guest list lays wide open our family trees for the rest of the community to dance and drink with, if they dare."

—COURTNEY PARKER
HOW TO EAT LIKE A SOUTHERNER
AND LIVE TO TELL ABOUT IT

A person doesn't have to live in the South to want to share good food with friends at the end of a warm day when the breeze is just right or to bask in the rewarding afterglow of a hard day's work in the garden. Southerners didn't invent these sorts of simple pleasures—we just refined them.

—CARLTON RILEY SMITH

NOW THAT WE KNOW WHAT SOUTHERN ENTERTAINING is, let's throw on a strand of pearls and get partying. As any real Pearl Girl knows, we wouldn't use plastic cups at a wedding, and we wouldn't wear a ball gown to tailgate (unless you're homecoming queen, of course). We Pearl Girls know that there's a season for everything, so when it's appropriate, we'll divide entertaining into three categories:

High-Falutin'—Weddings, bar and bat mitzvahs, debutante balls, masquerades, and other fancy-dress events. This is the time to really shine: your best jewelry, full makeup, and of course, your best behavior, though we know you Pearl Girls are ladies even at a pig roast.

Falutin'—Cocktail parties, sit-down dinners, and other events that don't require your finest attire, but always require your best behavior. You'll still be shining like the Pearl you are, but you can let down that well-coifed hair a little bit.

Just Falutin' Around—Pool parties, picnics, tailgating, cards with the ladies, and any event featuring sweaty men. (And I don't mean a strip club—we're ladies, remember!) You can let your hair all the way down, though naturally it'll still be perfectly combed and conditioned.

Making a List and
Checking It Twice (or Thrice)

The best party planning I ever did was with a professional caterer. She had lists of everything: grocery list for the menu; shopping list for the décor; lists of guests who were definite, probable, or negative; lists of the pots and pans she'd need; lists of the linens she would set out; and lists of the serveware she'd need, including serving spoons and forks. She even had a list of all the lists! Her most important list was her to-do list: what to do a month, week, and day before the party, as well as what to do on the day of the party itself. For those of us who can't keep our days of the week straight, lists are all-important. I like to keep a neat folder with all my lists so that I know what I've done and need to do every minute.

A PEARL GIRL KNOWS

A Southern Girl knows that the best way to approach a party is to imagine that her mother-in-law (and all of her ex- and future mothers-in-law) are coming.

If you have a fancy pocket computer, this is the time to dig it out, but if you're anything like me, you'll forget how to use it and miss your important dates. If you have any technological doubts (and who over the age of twelve doesn't?) it's probably best to stick to good old pen and paper and put everything in a party-planning binder or notebook.

For a High-Falutin' blowout event, the lists are particularly important. When you're juggling caterers, florists, musicians, and banquet halls, as well as the special needs of your guests, the lists will be your salvation (especially if, like me, you'd forget your head if it weren't attached to your neck). You'll probably have a large guest list that's hard to keep straight, so have a space next to each name to check whether they've sent in an RSVP, and if so whether they're yes, no, or maybe. You also might want to leave a space for notes to yourself to use at other stages in party planning: if Aunt Edna sits near Aunt Pearl, the fur's gonna fly; Miss Taylor won't eat meat or dairy; Reverend Walker hates alcohol, so don't put him next to Bob "Chug-a-Lug" Luger. Be careful to note what (and whom) each guest is allergic to.

When planning a High-Falutin' party, it's especially important to have a master list of important dates: When does the caterer need a deposit and final menu selections? When do you meet with the florist? When do you need to reserve the band and provide a song list? Professionals often don't

Goodness Gracious!

You can take a Pearl Girl from the South, but you can't take the South from her mouth. During a 2002 interview in a Hollywood restaurant, Julia Roberts said, "Quite a highfalutin' dealio they've got going on here."

have time to give you a reminder call, so don't let those dates slip past and miss an important detail in your event.

For most Falutin' and Just Falutin' Around parties, you don't need to be nearly as rigid. You'll have a smaller guest list, and you'll likely not be dealing with professionals who have deadlines. It's still important to have your shopping, guest, and to-do lists ready. Don't wait until an hour before the backyard barbecue (on a Sunday in a dry county) to remember that you need beer.

From Grilling-and-Chilling to Ballroom Milling . . . Know Your Party and Your Theme

What kind of party are you throwing? Cocktail party, ladies' lunch, barn dance, debutante tea, baby shower, barbecue, bar mitzvah, wedding, clambake, hoedown, masquerade, covered-dish supper, banquet . . . It may sound so obvious that you may not even consider your type of party, but I've been to cocktail parties with enough food to be banquets, and banquets without enough nibbles to feed an anorexic rabbit. If the hostess had figured out her goal before she started, these problems would never have come up.

When planning your party, always keep your goals in mind. If you want to showcase your beautiful garden, an evening cocktail party won't do you any good, but a garden party, cookout, or Sunday brunch alfresco will be perfect. If you want to welcome friends to your home, an evening housewarming or cocktail party will be a good choice. If you are too harried to plan a four-course meal, a covered-dish supper will suit you much better than a meal you have to cook yourself. If you want to help Vicky through a rough divorce . . . well, leave the men behind and bring the wine (and whine). Keep your goals in mind, and how much time and money you're willing to spend, and you'll find that choosing your party is easy.

French Connection

Twenty years ago, I met and married the love of my life, and since he was a chef, I got a two-for-one deal! We love throwing theme parties, and one of the best we've held was "French Night." Our guests dined on French Onion Soup, Chicken Cordon Bleu, and Bombe Glacée (Baked Alaska to you and me). And, as if that food could get any better, each course was accompanied by a superb French wine, and French music played softly in the background throughout the meal.

After dinner, my husband took our guests on a tour of the French Riviera and wine country with a quiz. Here are a few questions he asked:

QUESTION: *Who was the star of* Gigi *that played a cameo role in* Chocolat?
ANSWER: *Leslie Caron*
QUESTION: *What is a soft, rich, fermented cheese?*
ANSWER: *Camembert*
QUESTION: *What is a classy dry white wine?*
ANSWER: *Pouilly-Fuissé*

The evening was a huge success, and our guests left with full tummies and full minds!

—Laura Geneux
  Foley, Alabama

Next, set your theme. I think that every party, from the simplest covered dish to the most elaborate retirement dinner, should have a theme. A theme helps you determine your decorations, your food, your music, even your guest list. You don't have to go overboard (though going overboard is something we Pearl Girls specialize in!). Just think of something unifying, such as a Western theme for a barbecue, a time-of-day gift theme for a bridal shower. (Make sure you bring an extra couple bottles of wine if you throw a bedtime bridal shower—future mother-in-law might collapse when she sees what's in some of the boxes), a color theme for a wedding, or a favorite love song for an anniversary or Valentine's Day.

The Chosen Few (or Many): The Guest List

The most vital element in any party atmosphere isn't the cheese plate or the ice sculpture—it's the people. Every party needs a good mix of people. Now, for a family event, you've got to invite everyone, but when you're talking about friends and neighbors, you've got a bit more choice. The people you invite must get along. This doesn't mean you have to invite best friends, but understand that the preacher may not have much in common with the Lynyrd Skynyrd fan.

If you invite people who have been "raised right," you shouldn't have any problem with personality clashes—the yellow dog Democrat can get along with the die-hard Republican if both know that you don't talk politics at a cocktail party.

Keep in mind, too, that sometimes differences can actually make a more interesting party. That wallflower might begin to shine if you have enough outgoing people to bring her out (and that Lynyrd Skynyrd fan might just end up playing guitar at one of those "new style" church services).

For a High-Falutin' or Falutin' party, it is vital that you have a set guest list and keep track of who has accepted or rejected your invitation. (Remember those lists!) Also remember that your uncle or tennis partner might not be offended if you leave their name off a dinner party list, but they will be hurt if they aren't invited to the wedding or retirement dinner, so check the list several times to make sure everyone is included. You'll need to plan in advance for seating, food, and beverages—and even so, it's better to plan for a couple of last-minute extras. For a Just Falutin' Around party, it's fine to just have a general idea of who is coming (if you've handed out flyers to the neighbors, you have no idea who might show up), but you will need a ball-park estimate of how many people might come so that you can buy what you need in advance.

Some Southern girls have a list of people they'll never invite again—the couple who argued about their sex life at a formal dinner or the man who got drunk and threw your mother's crystal goblets in the fire. I don't really enjoy having a hard-and-fast list—we all deserve a second chance—but it is good to keep potential disasters and conflicts in mind.

In the past, the gender balance at parties was considered vital. A hostess would panic if a man dropped out of a dinner at the last moment, leaving her with a "spare" woman. To me, it's much more important that you think your guests will like each other and have some common interests. Pearl Girls can handle themselves these days without a man to hang on to—but of course, they still make nice accessories.

Keep those close to you in mind, but bring in new faces. Pearl Girls know that the people at a good party are like the people in the South—a mix of good old-timers and some fun new people to spice things up. My goodness, maybe that's why living in the South sometimes feels like it's Mardi Gras all year long!

Location, Location, Location

The perfect location for a Southern party is, of course, the home. If you have a large and elegant home, even a large High-Falutin' party is appropriate. Usually, though, the home is too small or not elegant enough for a High-Falutin' party. Book the location well in advance—at least three to six months for an evening event and at least one month for a morning event. (Keep in mind, however, that some special locations may have a very long wait.) You will need to tour several locations before deciding on one. Country clubs, banquet halls, historic homes, restaurants, and botanical gardens are traditional locations, and will most likely have professional staffers who have the experience to help you, but you can also often rent nontraditional locations such as art galleries and libraries. Be sure to visit at the same time of day that you'll be hosting your event—the sunlit hall may be beautiful during the day but may look dark and dingy at night, and that drab room may just start to sparkle when it's lit with candlelight.

A PEARL GIRL KNOWS

Sometimes, the home is the star of the party itself. We Southerners love our homes, and a truly special one can make every Southern heart glad.

For a successful booking, keep a checklist with the questions you need to ask for each location you tour. If you know which questions to ask in advance, you won't be intimidated by an experienced manager, and you'll feel more comfortable that you've made the right choice. If the manager doesn't want to sit down and answer your questions, run as fast as your little heels will carry you—if he isn't cooperative when he's trying to sell you on the space, imagine what he'll be like when he has your money. This may seem like a long list, but you'll feel much better knowing you can kick your feet back with a glass of sweet tea and let someone else worry about the event!

❏ How many people can be comfortably be seated in the location?
❏ How far in advance must I book?
❏ What deposit is required, and under what conditions will it be returned to me?

❏ What is the personality of the manager or party coordinator? How reachable is he or she, and how willing is he or she to work with me?

❏ What control do I have over the décor? Can I bring my own flowers, napkins, or other things of importance to me?

❏ Must the food be ordered from the facility, or may I bring it in? If I can bring it in, what is the procedure for food delivery, refrigeration, heating, and serving?

❏ Will I need to hire servers, and, if so, what facilities will be provided for them?

❏ Will I have a private dressing room for the bride or guest of honor?

❏ What is the tipping policy?

❏ What facilities are available for the musicians, and what dancing space is available?

For a Falutin' or Just Falutin' Around party, we Pearl Girls always want to welcome people into our homes, though sometimes, we also enjoy meeting at a restaurant, a park, or another location, in which case scouting out the setting is just as important as it is with a High-Falutin' party. More often, though, we like to open our own doors to welcome friends and neighbors. When the location is your

A PEARL GIRL KNOWS

Make sure you do all your home maintenance jobs well in advance of guests arriving. Your home might be beautiful, but if your air conditioners don't work, it's not beautiful enough to distract your guests from the Mississippi heat in August.

home, set aside the rooms or garden space where you want to entertain ahead of time. (And arrange a backup space in case of rain, even if the morning looks beautiful. As they say, if you don't like the weather in the South, wait ten minutes.) Be aware of the crowd size and traffic flow, and move furniture and cushions out of the way as appropriate. Be sure that you have enough table space for the food and drinks (and enough chairs for the heavy drinkers). I like to set aside another table (or better yet, another room) for desserts. Your guests will feel that they're being pampered, and the traffic flow to the food will be much eased.

Goodness Gracious!

It's always nice to set aside a room where women can gossip and tend to their clothes and makeup in peace. A perfect room is the boudoir. In medieval Europe, noblewomen often had a small cubbyhole or corner where they would go to be alone. Men being men, they would refer to this room as the boudeur, from the French for "sulking" or "pouting." The word became boudoir in English, but let's hope your guests don't do too much crying there—it'll ruin that makeup.

Ladies May Not Talk about Money, But They Know How to Budget

There's an ugly subject that should not be brought up during a party but has to be brought up before it begins—money. If you're Bill Gates and want to share the wealth, by all means decorate your cakes in gold leaf and break out the finest

Christmas at
Magnolia Manor

Christmastime is the ultimate season for events at our white brick plantation home, Magnolia Manor. It is a tradition to begin the parties of December with all rooms, hallways, doors, and stairways decorated with themed Christmas trees. (We even have one in the bathroom!) Lit reindeer lead the way up our winding driveway to the garlanded and wreath-covered porches and balconies. Each of the fifteen windows on the front of the house is lit by candles. We throw open the front and side doors to welcome people in, where they are met by the smells of scented candles, potpourri, hot mulled cider, and tablefuls of Christmas treats. It gives me a thrill to know that I will have a small part in bringing the Christmas joy into someone's heart as they visit our home.

We have trees all over the house, and these are just a few of them:

- **Anniversary Tree:** A tree in honor of our December anniversary decorated with white ornaments and draped with white fabric and flower petals.
- **Travels Tree:** A gold-and-burgundy tree decorated with gold ornaments collected during many years of travels.
- **Living Room Trees:** Two trees decorated with silver poinsettias, silver garlands and balls, and silver musical instruments.
- **Dining Room Trees:** Two trees decorated with gold poinsettias, gold garlands and ropings, gold balls, angels, and fruit.
- **Family Room Tree:** An old-fashioned family tree decorated with yards of ribbon and heirlooms from three generations.
- **Kitchen Tree:** Decorated with candy canes, cooking ornaments, and cookie cutters. Lots of Christmas tins surround the base.
- **Alma Mater Tree:** University of Tennessee Tree decorated with bright orange bubble lights, orange balls, and Tennessee memorabilia.

- **Coke Tree**: *Decorated with bright red lights and Coke ornaments from the present and past. A Coke village is under the tree.*
- **NASCAR Tree**: *Black-and-white flags adorn this tree, as well as NASCAR ornaments and years of racing memorabilia from Daytona and Talladega.*

As you can see, we go out of our way to entertain our guests and welcome them into our home. Our gatherings over the years have ranged from tea luncheons with friends to formal sit-down dinners with large groups, school tours, cookie exchanges, Scout troop tours, Sunday school parties, fund-raisers for the Murfreesboro Philharmonic Orchestra, swinging with the Red Hat Society, open houses for the whole neighborhood, and treasured family reunion times. Christmas is a special season, and I'm glad to open our home and our hearts to everyone. I thank God for giving us His Son and this season, and for being the recipient of His gift of hospitality.

—Aletha Mai Wright
  Murfreesboro, Tennessee

champagne with no thought of tomorrow. We mere mortals who have house payments, however, need to budget.

For a High-Falutin' party, the budget is particularly important. Cost can easily overrun by thousands of dollars if you do not keep a rein on your spending. Make a list of what you'll realistically need for the party beforehand: flowers, food, room, entertainment, decorations, gifts, and so on. Try to get a rough estimate from florists, photographers, and caterers of what their services cost. Then, swallow hard and figure out what you are able to spend on each item. You may not be able to afford orchids and caviar, but it's better to have a joyful party with carnations and onion dip than to blow your poor daughter's inheritance.

Goodness Gracious!

In 1895, George Washington Vanderbilt III opened the 250-room Biltmore Estate in Asheville, North Carolina. The home, which featured sixty-five fireplaces, had an indoor pool and bowling alley. The main dining table could seat sixty-four guests, and a typical dinner had eight courses and required fifteen utensils. In case the guests felt crowded, the estate was on a 125,000-acre spread, complete with gardens and carriage paths. I guess some Southerners don't need a budget for entertaining.

Even for a Falutin' or Just Falutin' Around party, it is a good idea to budget in advance. Little extras like candles, flowers, and candies can be surprisingly expensive, so plan ahead.

Once you have set your budget, stick to it. It's not easy—who doesn't love to shop, shop, shop—but it's a necessity, sugar. Always give yourself a little wiggle room—set your budget for each item at 10 percent less than you can afford to spend. That way, if your guests drink more than you expected, you won't have to take out a second mortgage on the Winnebago.

From Catfish to Caviar, Frog's Legs to Flounder: The Menu

For a High-Falutin' party, keep your caterer's dates for setting the menu in mind. For any party (High-Falutin' to Just Falutin' Around), get your menu set three weeks ahead. Keep in mind what's in season, and always have a backup plan. The key to a good menu—whether it's cocktail nibbles, a big buffet spread, or a formal sit-down dinner—is balance. I once went to a covered dish where four out of ten people brought deviled eggs. Keep in mind temperatures, colors, and textures, and try to get a little of each. That nice, crisp raw salad

The holiday table is never considered complete if you can't fill up at least one separate table with food—baked turkey, baked duck, baked ham, dressing with giblet gravy, potato salad, cranberry sauce, chow chow, mustard and turnip greens, corn bread, yeast rolls, coconut cake, jelly cake, caramel cake, pecan pies, sweet potato pies, ambrosia and fruit cake.

—Kathy Starr,
  The Soul of Southern Cooking

would go great with a pot roast, but would be boring next to crudités.

Keep the various diets in mind. Some people won't eat any meat, and some will eat nothing but. Try to have at least something for everyone if you can. Pearl Girls don't burden their hosts with their special diets (their mothers taught them that it was better to be a bit hungry than to make their hostess change the menu), so it's up to you to keep different diets in mind.

SOUTHERN TRANSLATION

progressive [prə gre´ siv] **adj**. *pertaining to a type of left-wing political thought;* **n**. *a dinner at which each course is eaten at a separate home.*

When you're figuring out how much to serve, too much is always better than too little. If lamb chops for twenty are stretching your budget too thin, it's better to serve a healthy portion of meatloaf than one skinny little chop per guest. Your guests will never know that you considered something "fancy," and they'll much rather see the plate piled high with well-made food, no matter how humble, than see an empty platter when they're still hungry. Keep in mind that what might fill up the stomach of a Pearl Girl might be considered dainty to others, particularly the menfolk. You might be eating leftovers for weeks—or better yet, stocking up the local homeless shelter—but your guests will feel well cared for, and they won't be embarrassed when they ask for seconds and nothing is left.

Four Ways to
Get the Grub on the Table

1. **Cooperative cooking.** *The meal planning and cooking are divided among guests. Guests usually bring food to one location. Cooperative cooking is great for family dinners or a group of close friends, but it isn't very well suited to a formal High-Falutin' party. For an occasion that lasts more than one day (such as a family reunion) cooperative cooking may be the only way to maintain your sanity.*

2. **Catering.** *Someone drops off the food (and sometimes even serves it on a silver platter). Perfect for High-Falutin' parties or for those of us who prefer not to cook. (I think there's a kitchen somewhere behind the living room, but I haven't visited for a while.)*

3. **Potluck.** *Everyone brings their favorite dish. Best for Just Falutin' Around parties. The key to a successful potluck is making sure that the dishes are balanced, so state in advance who should bring a green salad, a dessert, meat or poultry, a starchy side dish, and so forth.*

4. **Do-it-yourself.** *The host provides and prepares all the food. Although this is suitable for any style of party, know your limits. If your idea of cooking is microwaving a burrito, a do-it-yourself formal dinner is probably a bit ambitious. Plan in advance, clear out your refrigerator, make sure you have not only the ingredients but the proper equipment as well, and make a list of everything you need to do and when you need to do it. And one last thing—you've got my admiration.*

A Tidewater Tradition

Girls raised in Tidewater, Virginia, were brought up with love and respect for ham biscuits, that delectable delicacy of paper-thin Virginia ham and small biscuits the size of fifty-cent pieces. From their mothers and grandmothers they learned that this special gourmet food was right for all kinds of entertaining. . . . In fact, a notable Virginia hostess loved to describe the occasion that brought President Theodore Roosevelt for a visit to the Virginia Governor's Mansion at the time her father, Andrew Jackson Montague, was governor. At the turn of the century, few if any state governors had expense accounts, and the costs of entertaining guests was an out-of-pocket matter for each individual governor. Governor and Mrs. Montague therefore decided that the appropriate refreshment for the president's reception was ham biscuits and champagne!

—Spotswood H. Jones
  Gloucester, Virginia

Ham Biscuits

> 2 cups all-purpose flour
> 2 teaspoons baking powder
> 1 heaping teaspoon baking soda
> 1 teaspoon salt
> ¼ cup plus 2 tablespoons vegetable shortening or lard (for a crispier biscuit, praise the lard)
> ⅔ cup buttermilk
> Slices of country ham so thin you can almost see through them (or substitute prosciutto cut by the people at the deli)

Preheat oven to 450 degrees F. Mix together the dry ingredients in a large bowl. Cut the shortening or lard into

Continues...

the dry ingredients until mixture looks like a coarse meal. Stir in the buttermilk. Turn the dough out onto a lightly floured surface and knead it a few times. Roll out the dough until it's ¼ to ½ inch thick (depending on your preference). Cut rounds with a small biscuit cutter and place them on cookie sheet. Bake for 8 to 10 minutes. When the biscuits are done, split them open, and eat as a sandwich with the ham between.

When planning the menu, plan the appropriate beverages, and the glasses and accessories you'll need to serve them. And keep in mind that even if the food fails, no one will care as long as there's enough booze around.

A PEARL GIRL KNOWS

A Pearl Girl without lipstick is like a Yankee without his lawyer. At cocktail parties, try to keep the nibbles small enough so the ladies won't have to ruin their lipstick.

If you're cooking your own meal, keep your sanity in mind. Pearl Girls need time to do their hair, sugar, so they don't want to be rushing around before their party starts. Make as many cook-ahead dishes as you can. At an event involving lots of nibbles, make sure that you don't have too many hot dishes—something that can be pulled out of the icebox at the last minute will save your sanity (not to mention that flawless complexion).

Cut to the Caterer

1. Get recommendations, but also taste the food. If a restaurant is catering, ask to taste the dishes the restaurant makes for parties, not the regular menu. Even if you love the restaurant's cheese soufflé, the cocktail meatballs may taste like cardboard.
2. Ask for a signed contract specifying when the food will be delivered, whether serving and serveware is included, what dishes and how much of each will be supplied.
3. Be prepared to give a deposit at the time of booking.
4. Have the caterer prepare for 10 percent more guests—you never know when Cousin Margaret and her family will come blowing into town and expect to be fed.
5. Know in advance what your caterer will need—kitchen counter space, refrigerators, setup area—so that there will be no last-minute surprises.
6. Know in advance whether your caterer will be cleaning up. Post-party, will you be soaking in a warm bath—or scrubbing the dishes?
7. Know who keeps the leftovers. That last piece of chocolate cake should belong to you, not the caterer's teenage son!

The Trimmings—Flowers and Music Fashioned for the Senses

Flowers make every party (from the simplest picnic to the most elegant wedding) special and memorable. If you are hosting a High-Falutin' party, you'll most likely use a florist. Choose your florist and your flowers well in advance.

When choosing a florist,

1. Get recommendations.
2. Ask about deposits and the circumstances under which you'll get your money back.
3. Have some idea of what you want in advance. You may not be able to name the types of flowers you want, but you should have a color scheme and style in mind.

Sample Menus— Balancing Tastes, Textures, and Temperatures

AUTUMN DINNER FOR EIGHT	LIGHT COCKTAIL BUFFET
Butternut squash soup	Cold asparagus wrapped in Smithfield ham
Roast pork tenderloin with root vegetables and steamed brussels sprouts	Hot mini cheese quiches
	Cold steamed shrimp with cocktail sauce
	Crudités platter with dips
Spinach salad	Hot mini-meatballs
Gingerbread with lemon sauce	Fresh berries

For your autumn menu, the only last-minute cooking is the steamed brussels sprouts. Put them on as your guests sit down to soup, and by the time you go back into the kitchen, all you have to do is take them out and toss them with a bit of butter and salt. For the cocktail buffet, just pop the quiches in an oven and the meatballs in a Crock-Pot, and you're ready. You don't want to be scrambling around at the last minute and chip one of those nails, after all!

4. Find out what the policy on substitutions is. If you have your heart set on lavender, know that your florist understands and respects your wishes.
5. Make it clear in advance whether the flowers will be delivered or picked up, and if they are going to be picked up, ask when they will be ready.
6. Find out when your florist will need access to the room, and be sure that you or someone else can let him in.

For a Falutin' or Just Falutin' Around party, you won't have a florist come into your house to decorate. If you don't arrange flowers yourself, you can pick up an arrangement at a florist or even at the local supermarket. Arranging flowers will save you money, however, and is surprisingly simple. You can even pick the flowers from your garden or a neighbor's. (Ask first, of course—don't sneak into the yard at midnight.)

1. Choose an interesting container. It doesn't have to be a vase, but it should be waterproof. (Your grandmother wouldn't appreciate water rings on her antique table.)
2. Cut florist foam to size, and place it in the container. The foam should be slightly higher than the edge of the container so that some flowers or greenery flow down the edge of the container.

3. Arrange your flowers first. Try to have a combination of open and closed flowers. For ideas, check several magazines or look at what the florists have out in their shops.
4. Add your filler. Greenery, baby's breath, and Queen Anne's lace are all excellent fillers and are not costly.

5. Try not to use too many different flowers. Your arrangement should be an elegant parlor, not a jumbled garage.
6. Add water, step back, and enjoy!

When setting your flowers out, keep your space in mind. You don't want Mrs. Tuttle's gown catching on a hanging branch. Short arrangements are nice for a tabletop. (Your guests should see each other, not a jumble of ferns.) For a buffet, go vertical, and set the flowers above the food and utensils.

A PEARL GIRL KNOWS

Don't forget that your guests will see every room in your house. A single bud in a vase looks beautiful in the washroom.

Flowers are always beautiful and elegant, but don't feel limited. A platter of fruits, a jumble of your collections, such as crystal pieces, ceramics, Christmas ornaments, or decorative containers, or even a dramatic candleholder all make beautiful centerpieces. For Christmas, you can wrap empty packages and set them around the table and room. For Easter, a dramatic Easter basket filled with decorated eggs looks wonderful.

The last touch is music. Choose a DJ, orchestra, or single musician, depending on your budget and the mood you want to set. A High-Falutin' party should ideally have live music of some kind, but a Falutin' or Just Falutin' Around

Christmas with a
First-Class First Lady

Laura Bush, wife of President George W. Bush and proud daughter of Midland, Texas, doesn't decorate the White House with the standard ribbons and bows. Instead, she lets each decoration reflect her personal passion—books. For Christmas 2003, she decorated the White House in a children's storybook theme. The characters from Little Women (the First Lady's favorite book as a child) grace one mantel in the East Room, and Harry Potter and his owl Hedwig (Mrs. Bush read all five books the summer before!) grace another. In the center of the room stands a replica of Willy Wonka's chocolate factory created by the White House pastry chef—let's hope the White House dogs, Barney and Spot, stayed away from its eighty pounds of chocolate! In the State Dining Room, characters from Alice's Adventures in Wonderland stood on the buffet table. (Since the Queen of Hearts was made of papier-mâché, she won't be ordering the heads chopped off of any foreign dignitaries.) In the Blue Room, an eighteen-foot Fraser fir was decorated with storybook character ornaments lent by her father-in-law's library. Hundreds of storybooks stood below the tree—Mrs. Bush has made it part of her mission as First Lady to encourage parents to read to children.

Your home may not be as impressive as the White House, and your holiday entertaining schedule not as hectic. (Goodness knows I have no plans to throw ten parties in ten days—how does she find any time to read?) But even so, you can follow the First Lady's example by having your decorations reflect your own interests. No matter what you care about, letting it show in your décor will give your home a special touch, and make it something your guests will remember.

party can get by with only your stereo. If you're playing your own music, set aside the music you want to hear ahead of time. Begin the party with medium volume, turn it down during a meal, and then turn it up again after dinner. For High-Falutin' and Falutin' parties, light jazz or classical is best in the background, and for a Just Falutin' Around party, anything goes! Expect to have some yo-yo rooting around in your music collection and playing that disco album you thought you gave away. Don't be embarrassed—it's all part of the fun.

Invitations: You Get Only One Chance to Make a First Impression

There was a time when an invitation meant one thing—a handwritten note requesting the honor of someone's presence. To real Pearl Girls, that's what an invitation still is. Southern girls know that that envelope is still an important part of social etiquette. Remember how much fun it was to get mail when you were a child? With enough effort and thoughtfulness, your guests can get that same thrill again.

A PEARL GIRL KNOWS

Want to take all the anticipation and joy from an invitation? Use an e-invitation! There's only one proper way to use e-mail to invite your friends to a party—don't.

The Serenading Groom

My Yankee girlfriend was getting married, and I should have known there'd be trouble when I received an invitation complete with registry information. (How tacky!)

The reception seemed like a classic Southern reception until you looked a bit harder. The groom's brother gave a tasteless toast. The groom was walking around with shirt untucked and his jacket nowhere to be seen. One of the bridesmaids was wearing jeans and hot-pink sneakers under her dress. The bride, unconcerned by any of this, was having a ball.

Then the DJ summoned the bride and her new husband to the dance floor, and he gave a verbal disclaimer. "Um, sorry, I don't want to offend anyone, but I've had an unusual request from the bride. In fact, I've never had this request or played this song for a wedding. Would the groom please come up here?" The groom grabbed a beer, chugged it, burped into the microphone, and began to sing along with the music. The song was "Why Don't We Get Drunk and ———" (Being a real Southern lady, I won't repeat the last word of the song, but you get the idea).

The bride laughed in delight, but we Pearl Girls thanked her parents and cleared out of there as fast as we could.

—Aimee Weaver
   Dunwoody, Georgia
   (but still a North Carolina girl at heart!)

Formal Invitations

If you're having a High-Falutin' party, such as a large wedding or other black tie affair, a formal, printed invitation is the best bet, and this kind of invitation will make even a Falutin' party special. Formal invitations are usually printed on cream or white colored paper, though the ink color is something you can choose. Keep in mind that printers will need at least four to six weeks to have the invitations ready for delivery. Though the invitation is printed, the guest's name, and the envelope, are written by hand with a fountain pen. Use the person's full title on the envelope, *Mr. Elvis Presley,* but only the name inside, *The King.*

Goodness Gracious!

Before the Civil War, instead of sending out paper invitations to wedding guests, it was common for young couples to invite friends and family by placing an advertisement in the local newspaper.

The formal invitation should be written in the third person, so "Deborah Ford requests the honor of your presence" is better than "Come on down, sugar." Punctuation is not used at the end of lines, but it is used within lines to separate the day from the date, and the city from the state. Only proper nouns are capitalized, with the exception of the year. Some people believe that the British spelling of words is preferable on a formal invitation (*honour* and *favour* instead of *honor* and *favor*). Since Pearl Girls aren't English, I don't see the sense of it. I figure if I'd get marked down for spelling a word in school, I don't need to be using it on an invitation. Whatever spelling usage you decide, be consistent.

Your invitations should state the following, in order:

- *The name of parents, hosts, or sponsors (the name of a real person is best, so* Mr. Bigshot, CEO of Multi-National Corp. *is better than* Multi-National Corp. *alone)*
- *The purpose of the invitation (requests the honor of your presence at a retirement party)*
- *The name of the honoree or honorees (in honor of devoted underling Jim Bob McGuigan)*
- *Date, with the year spelled out (January 1, Two thousand twenty-five)*
- *Name of location (Hoity Toity Country Club)*
- *Locale (Pigeon Spit, Arkansas)*

The rules for formal invitations may seem daunting, but there's one easy way to make sure you follow them: Ask! The man or woman who's printing your invitations has seen hundreds of them, and knows the rules better than you do. Don't be embarrassed by your questions. If you feel like a fool asking a simple question, imagine how you'll feel when a couple of hundred people see an error that could have easily been avoided.

A PEARL GIRL KNOWS

Have two people who have never seen your invitations proofread them. Don't send out five hundred invitations only to have someone call and tell you the bride's name is misspelled.

Informal Invitations

For a Falutin' or Just Falutin' Around party, the only rule that applies to an invitation is Have fun! When you're on your next vacation, pick up a bunch of fun postcards, and use them for your next party—better yet let the location of your postcard set the theme for your party, a luau for your Hawaii postcards or a mountain hootenanny for your Gatlinburg cards. Or write a silly poem and put it on some fancy paper. For a Christmas party, write the invitation on simple red or green paper, then wrap each invitation in some fun Christmas paper and a bow, and hand-deliver it to your guests. For a party with Asian food, fold each invitation into an origami swan. For a birthday party, scan a baby picture of the honoree into your computer (or get your twelve-year-old neighbor to do it if you don't know how); then print out as many invitations using the picture as you want. It might even be fun to leave off the name of the honoree and let your friends guess who the baby is.

With informal invitations, your imagination is your only limit. And don't forget that the delivery can be as fun as the invitation itself. If you're having a Halloween party for your

While creative stationery can make a good party invitation, try to stay away from anything with a black border. In Victorian times, upper-class women used high-grade stationery with a black border during a period of mourning (and those ladies could carry on their mourning for years).

neighbors, why not pay some local children to dress up and deliver the invitations? Or dress up as a wicked witch (or a sexy little bunny rabbit if you can get away with it) and bring the invitations around yourself!

Just have fun and let your imagination go. Your invitation sets the mood for the party, and if you use your head and a bit of creativity, people will practically be begging to be your guest.

Pearl Girl Parties

Getting together with men is fun, but getting together with the ladies is even better! Whether we're cooing over baby gifts or sipping tea at a garden party, Pearl Girls love to spend time together.

We've all heard of hen parties, garden parties, baby and bridal showers, bridge luncheons, and ladies' nights (pass those Jell-O shooters!), but a Pearl Girl party lets you enjoy your girlfriends and celebrate your Southern heritage.

Dress code is sundresses, white gloves, and (naturally) pearls. The food is pimento cheese and cucumber sandwiches, ham biscuits,

Continues...

deviled eggs, and other Southern treats. Top it off with iced tea or mint juleps. The best part is not the food, though, but sharing your Southern heritage. Have each woman bring a story to share about the South or her Southern heritage. It can be anything from a list of what she loves about growing up Southern (fireflies, screen doors, corn bread crumbled up in buttermilk, watermelon straight from the patch . . .) to an Uncle Remus story to the tale of how Great-great-grandma Lexie hid the family silver from the Yankees (while Great-granddaddy was too busy hiding the guns). Whatever your guests choose to share, every guest will be a little richer for the hearing.

Deviled Eggs for Heavenly Ladies

> 6 hard-boiled eggs, peeled
> ¼ cup mayonnaise (the real stuff, please)
> 1 teaspoon prepared mustard
> Salt and pepper to taste
> Paprika

Cut the eggs in half and remove yolks. In a small bowl, mash the yolks well, and add mayonnaise, mustard, salt, and pepper. Stir well, and taste the mixture for consistency and flavor. (Add a bit more mayonnaise if it is too dry.) You can pipe the filling into the whites with a pastry bag, but if you're like me, you'll just spoon it right back in. Sprinkle the eggs with paprika.

For variety, you can spice up the recipe with a little cayenne or Worcestershire, substitute cider vinegar for the prepared mustard, or sprinkle fresh chives on top instead of paprika. Some folks even add a bit of smoked salmon, relish, or a flavorful cheese to the mix.

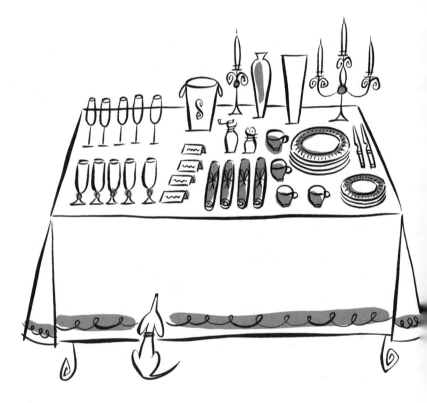

CHAPTER 5

The Week Before

There is a grand tradition known as "Southern hospitality." Southerners are renown for their courteous treatment of others. But the truest form of hospitality goes beyond common courtesy. It is ethical, compassionate treatment of others.

—CRISWELL FREEMAN
  SOUTHERN WISDOM

Become so wrapped up in something that you forget to be afraid.

—LADY BIRD JOHNSON
  KARNACK, TEXAS

A Borrower Be . . . Getting Everything Together

If you are hosting a High Falutin' party, it's time to contact everyone from the caterer to the musicians to make sure that everything is in order and to answer any last-minute questions. You might be afraid that you are pestering them, but don't worry—if they are professionals, they will be ready to help. Since you're a real Pearl Girl, you know that honey will catch those little caterer flies—ask if they need any help from you, not whether they've gotten their sorry behinds in shape yet.

If you are using any special item (it's your grandparents' anniversary, and you want to use the lace tablecloth they received as a wedding gift, or you've made personalized party favors for your guests), drop it off at your party location and be sure to clear it with the party coordinator or manager first. Try to set aside everything that you will need on the big day, or better yet arrange it in place. No matter how well you've planned for a High Falutin' event, on the day of the party you'll be rushing around getting your nails done, finding the cake that was somehow misplaced by the waiters, and picking up Cousin Rene and her eight kids from the airport. Any details that you can take care of in advance will spare your sanity when it's time for the big event.

For a Falutin' or Just Falutin' Around party, it's time to get everything together. I don't have one linen closet or china cabinet—I have dozens all over town! In the South, entertaining is a family affair, so I know that if I need a chafing dish or extra plates, I can raid the homes of family and friends. This is the time to beg and borrow, and drive on over and pick everything up.

Kitchen Capers—What You'll Need to Keep Everything Clean, Crisp, and Classy

- ☐ Cleanser, dishwashing liquid, and dishwasher detergent.
- ☐ Aluminum foil and plastic wrap.
- ☐ About twice as many garbage bags as you think you'll need.
- ☐ Aprons. KISS THE COOK (or KISS MY GRITS, if you're sassy) motto optional.
- ☐ Matches.
- ☐ Paper towels (plus a few rolls for the toddlers and the tipsy).
- ☐ Pot holders.
- ☐ Kitchen towels (since everyone will end up in the kitchen no matter how much you plan, replace those stained, torn, and generally unsightly old towels with something presentable).
- ☐ Sponges and scouring pads.
- ☐ Several sizes of Ziploc bags.
- ☐ Fire extinguisher. Especially if you've invited me to cook anything.
- ☐ Did I mention pearls?

A PEARL GIRL KNOWS

Stick your to-do list on your refrigerator, and consult it every time you hit the New York Super Fudge Chunk. (That should be New Orleans Super Fudge Chunk, honey, because we Southerners love to eat as much as those New Yorkers love their stock market!)

It's in the Presentation . . . Southern Style

Maybe we got it at our wedding, maybe we inherited it, or maybe we just picked it up ourselves, but Pearl Girls treasure their china, crystal, and flatware. And we love to get it out for any old reason. Maybe it's because we know that that boring old chicken breast sure tastes a lot better eaten off bone china with a La Regence silver fork. Or maybe we Pearl Girls just like to feel like the princesses we are every day.

For a High-Falutin party, only the best that you can afford will do. When you book a country club or a restaurant, check on the quality of their tableware. If the lemon pie is luscious, but the spoon is dinted and dinged, your party won't be everything that it should be. Some venues will allow you to bring your own serving pieces. If so, be sure that everything will be returned in good shape (and preferably clean) by asking everyone from the waitstaff to your hairdresser about the reputation of the venue. If there's any chance that a couple of pieces of antique silver will go walking, use what the restaurant or club owns. A better option in this case is selecting a caterer who will bring quality serving pieces. Your guests will be treated well, and you won't have to

You're on the Ten-Yard Line— Time Table

1. Shop for kitchen staples at least one week ahead of time: coffee (leaded and unleaded), flour and baking supplies, jarred spices, frozen fruit or vegetables.
2. Shop for wine and liquor at least a week ahead of time.
3. Pick up serving pieces, linens, and anything else you're borrowing six days ahead of time. Give the lender a compliment on her hair, nails, or clothes. (Even if she opens the door in a housedress and curlers, you can find something nice to say.)
4. Six days ahead of time, finish any nonperishable decorations, such as place cards and potpourri.
5. Five days ahead of time, prepare any frozen foods.
6. Five days ahead of time, press and neatly fold your linens.
7. Get that Botox! Those injections take two to five days to take effect.
8. Three days ahead, shop for and prepare any foods that can be refrigerated.
9. Three days ahead of time, get your manicure and pedicure.
10. If you have space, three days ahead, set aside any silver, plates, and serving pieces that you'll need. Get out that polish and the elbow grease if you see any tarnish. When everything is ready for use, set it aside, and cover with a clean sheet.
11. Two days before, shop for perishables.
12. Two days before, have a "dress rehearsal." Does your wardrobe need cleaning or pressing? Do you have jewelry and stockings?
13. Two days ahead of time, give the white glove treatment to everything but the kitchen. The kitchen will get dirty while you're

rushing around peeling, chopping, boiling, and burning. Don't wrinkle those pretty hands doing double cleaning duty.

14. The day before, pick up the ice, the keg, the flowers, salad greens, and anything else that you haven't picked up ahead of time.

15. The day before, marinate the meat, chop the veggies, prepare the centerpieces, and clean up that kitchen. (You may not mind the four-day-old cereal remnants in the sink, but your guests probably will.)

16. The day of, relax, get your hair done, and congratulate yourself on your fine party planning (or, in the real world, do the ten things that have slipped your mind).

worry about the wrath of your Aunty Patty when her favorite oval vegetable plate comes back chipped. If your High-Falutin' party is in your home, dig out the silver (and get rid of the tarnish), polish your plates, and dust your crystal.

Southern girls transplant well and blossom in a new location. We take with us a bit of the South wherever we go. The seasons change almost imperceptively in Hawaii, but at my home colorful faux leaves and mums abound starting in October. Friends always look forward to our Happy Fall, Y'all party. We serve lau lau, sushi, and sashimi along with our fried chicken, ham, and deviled eggs. We love to bring a bit of the South—and a bit of the season—right here to the land of aloha.

—Sonya Richter-Smith
  Honolulu, Hawaii

When I have a Falutin' party in my home, I like to serve the food buffet style. If you can't afford a waitstaff—and who can!—it keeps you at the table with your guests rather than serving. Still, just because the food is served buffet style doesn't mean that I don't break out my best! Pearl Girls know that any occasion is a good enough occasion to use their finest, just like any trip out of the house is occasion enough to wear lipstick. You wouldn't go out wearing scruffy old sweatpants, so why should your food come out on a beat-up everyday platter?

If you're a Pearl Girl who isn't lucky enough to have the goods yet, take heart. Select a china pattern; then start collecting. Collect your party gear like you collect clothes—start with a few basic pieces, and then get the extras to complement your basic patterns. Don't be afraid to borrow what you don't have, especially if you're having an event for the whole family—your aunt Bertha will be more than happy to have a chance to show off her gorgeous serving platter.

Many china manufacturers have "starter kits" that will have the most commonly used pieces for place settings of four or eight. If these are too expensive, start with a couple of pieces, and buy more when you can afford to. For each place setting, you'll want to start with at least a dinner plate and a salad or dessert plate. Then, move on to a bread plate, a soup plate, a soup bowl, and a teacup and saucer. A basic pattern that will last through the years is better than something hip or flashy (just like a good old Southern belle is better than some globe-trotting Yankee fashion victim), and it will blend better with accessories as times and tastes change.

SOUTHERN TRANSLATION

porcelain [pôr´ sə lin] n. *strong, translucent, and difficult to stain, this is the "queen of ceramics," and justifiably handed down through the generations.*

bone china [bōn´ chī´ nə] n. *the addition of bone ash makes this china a beautiful, creamy white.*

earthenware [ʉrth´ ən wer] n. *made from less refined clays and fired at a lower temperature, this is suitable for everyday use.*

glass [glas] n. *made from tempered glass, these make great accent pieces for a place setting (combine a china dinner plate with a colorful glass salad plate).*

paper [pā´ pər] n. *suitable for picnics and rowdy five-year-olds, these are as welcome at a High-Falutin' party as a monkey at a debutante ball.*

Goodness Gracious!

Tired of setting out all those different silver pieces? Festival Before Forks is celebrated every Christmas at Boar's Head Inn in Charlottesville, Virginia, is a sixteenth-century English banquet. Before dinner, the staff confiscates all utensils. Sure beats trying to figure out how to use the olive fork!

Once you have your china, move on to the silver and stemware. For your flatware, you'll need to choose sterling (starting around $250 per place setting), silver plate (starting around $40 per place setting), or stainless (starting around $15 per place setting). Any choice is appropriate for casual to formal entertaining.

For your glassware, leaded glass is generally considered the best, and is the most expensive. Clear glasses will let you have the most variety in what you serve (ever seen red wine in a blue glass?), and a simple and tasteful design is your best choice.

A PEARL GIRL KNOWS

Moonshine can be served in your grandmother's old fruit jars, though remember to put the lid on after each service or the dog might pass out from the fumes.

Floral china goes well with etched or cut crystal and more ornate silverware. Simple china goes well with clear crystal and clean architectural flatware. Feel free, though, to ignore these basic rules. A real Pearl Girl knows that rules are made to be broken. Keep in mind the Pearl Girl principle of elegant simplicity, and you can't go wrong with any combination.

If you have your basics, you can go crazy. There's a flatware or china piece for absolutely everything you might want. It's nice to have butter knives, butter spreaders, serving spoons and forks, ladles, and sugar spoons in your flatware. But there are also cream soup spoons, gumbo spoons, bourbon spoons, five o'clock spoons, asparagus tongs, apple knives, olive forks, lemon forks and strawberry forks. If you're lucky enough to inherit these pieces, feel free to use them for different things. Cream soup spoons are great for ice cream, for instance, and asparagus tongs can be used to pick up just about any small food item. In your china, you'll want a couple of oval serving dishes and vegetable plates. Feel free to be creative with your pieces. That gravy boat is perfect for chocolate sauce or salad dressing. And if you have some pieces that don't "match," go ahead and use them! Your silver may have various monograms (especially if you're picking up extra pieces at flea markets), but that just makes it more interesting. And those serving pieces may be from a different pattern, but as long as they complement your basic décor, they add interest to a table. In fact, if you use pieces that aren't perfectly matched, your table will be a perfect blend of tradition and new, just like us Pearl Girls!

SOUTHERN TRANSLATION

sterling [stur´ ling] **n.** *a combination of 92.5 percent silver and 7.5 percent base metal, usually copper.*
silver plate [sil´ vər plāt] **n.** *a base coat (a combination of nickel, copper, and zinc) coated with silver.*
stainless steel [stan´ lis stēl] **n.** *durable metal alloy, often with 18 percent chromium for strength and 10 percent nickel for shine.*

A Just Falutin' Around party does not technically require your finest tableware, but it does require a good-looking table. For any indoor party, it's preferable to use real glassware, linens, and plates (though you can also collect interesting, high-quality plastic plates for an unusual presentation). Disposable plates or cups are best left for pool parties and tailgating. (Your grandmother would probably not appreciate it if you put her finest on a picnic table.) You don't have to get out that lead crystal for every cocktail party, but you shouldn't use plastic cups unless it is absolutely necessary. (A group of hyperactive five-year-olds probably shouldn't be running around with real glass.) Discount stores often carry glasses for less than a dollar apiece, so you can put inexpensive glassware away for your large cocktail parties (and for everyday use if your husband's glass ends up on the floor more often than on the coaster). Paper cocktail napkins are, of course, suitable for even a High-Falutin' party (no Pearl Girl wants condensation dripping on her silk gown), but real cloth napkins are better at the table.

Don't Forget the Tablecloth!

A tablecloth is to a table what jewelry is to a woman—it completes the picture. For High-Falutin' and Falutin' parties, tablecloths are absolutely mandatory. A good tablecloth will add softness to the hard elements (the china, crystal, and flatware) on your table or sideboard. It also protects your fine furniture or (if you're still using that beer-stained card table from college) hides what you don't have.

Just like with your tableware, it's best to start with the basics. Formal tables are traditionally set with a white or cream damask cloth, and it's best to start with this piece since it's the most versatile. For a High-Falutin' party, these colors are the best choice. For a Falutin' party, you have more choice in colors, but a white or cream tablecloth is like a little black dress—it won't be wrong in any situation, and you can always dress it up. If you have a fine dining table that you'd like to show off, a lace, rather than a solid, piece of cloth will let your guests see the table surface.

A PEARL GIRL KNOWS

At a High-Falutin' party, aim for symmetry when you're setting the table. Begin with the centerpiece and work your way out. For a less formal table, aim for festiveness and fun with different colors and patterns.

A tablecloth should be ironed before use. Always iron on the "wrong" side of damask to protect the sheen. When storing, try to roll, rather than fold, the cloth to avoid rot at the edges of the cloth. Old wrapping paper tubes can help preserve your cloths.

For a Just Falutin' Around party, feel free to use something crazy. Scarves, quilts, bedspreads, even cloth wall hangings (but probably not Granddaddy's old bear skin complete with eyes!) make for interesting décor and conversation. Or, get a roll of cheap brown paper, and roll it across the table for those messy crab, lobster, or shrimp dinners. Supply your guests with crayons for a little extra fun!

Goodness Gracious!

Before the use of the fork became widespread, napkins were used to wipe greasy fingers after taking food from the common pot (and for wiping the teeth at the end of the meal!). Although we Pearl Girls know to always keep our napkins in our laps during the meal, it was once the custom to drape it over the shoulder like a shawl.

Once you have your basic table cover, napkins and place mats can dress up the table (at a High-Falutin', Falutin', or Just Falutin' Around party). Different fabrics and colors can enliven even the simplest tablecloth. Manufactured napkin rings are available in just about any shape and material you could want, or make your own from plain ribbons, flowers, ivy, twine, small beads, or berries. Be sure if you raid the yard for holly, flowers, and greenery that you get rid of any insect hitchhikers before you use them on the table—nothing ruins the salad faster than a grasshopper coming out of the napkins. And keep in mind that gun shells are never acceptable, even if they killed the main course!

A PEARL GIRL KNOWS

For outdoor entertaining, always windproof your table. Bungee cords and grommets keep the tablecloth in place in the breeze.

Candles, Candy, and Canapés...
Remember the Details

Pearl Girls know that you can buy the best cut of meat at the butcher's, but if you don't serve it with the right trimmings, no one is going to come back for seconds. The trimmings at a party are those little details that keep 'em coming back for more. Details are important at any party—High-Falutin', Falutin', or Just Falutin' Around. If you are hosting a High-Falutin' party outside your home, check with the party coordinator or manager about what details you can supply yourself. Candles and decorations can add a special touch to any location.

A PEARL GIRL KNOWS

Avoid any artificial scents—air fresheners or scented candles. Hose down your dog and your husband. If all else fails, keep a pan of water and cinnamon on a low boil in the cold months, and scatter a natural potpourri in the warmer months.

Candles set the mood and make even the most run-down shack look good. Keep in mind, though, that these are only good for evening parties. For morning parties, bunches of flowers or fresh greenery can enliven the room. And whatever you do, make sure you put those candles in a place where your guests won't easily bump them. Hot-wax treatments should be administered only by professionals, sweetie.

A great way to set the mood is to light your guests' way into the party. Set out inexpensive bags weighted down by sand, and put a small votive candle in each. Just be sure to moisten the bags first. A visit by the fire department might add some excitement to your party, but not the kind of excitement Pearl Girls want. If you want something more interesting, be creative with your containers. Small pumpkins at Halloween, old cans pierced with dozens of holes (an icepick is good for this), or old ceramic pots also make great containers for your outdoor lighted walkway.

Rules for Waxing Poetic— Burning Candles without Burning Down the House

1. Keep candles away from drafts.
2. Use a snuffer to extinguish a flame—blowing can disperse soot and wax.
3. Always use an appropriate candleholder. I know that huge pillar looks like it can't possibly damage your table—but you don't want to find a pool of wax after a tiring evening and too many cocktails.
4. If wax does splash on wood, glass, or metal furniture, freeze it to harden (a Ziploc bag full of ice does the trick nicely), and then peel it away.
5. Trim wicks until they are only ¼ inch long. Shorter wicks mean less soot.
6. If your tablecloth is covered in wax, place a paper bag on the splash, and then iron (on an ironing board, honey, not your antique table!). The bag should absorb the wax.

Once your guests are inside, don't let the little details end. Set out small dishes of candy or other treats (homemade is best, but your guests will appreciate store-bought, too) throughout the entertaining area. If you have any interesting old containers, this is a great time to use them. That collection of fruit-shaped jelly servers that you never use would be great for hard candy, and those compotes someone gave you for your wedding would be a great showcase for individually wrapped homemade caramels. Have an ashtray from every state park? Fill them with tiny chocolates—it's better for your lungs than smoking and makes a great conversation starter for shy guests.

A PEARL GIRL KNOWS

Lost wineglasses are always a problem. These days, decorative "wine savers" are available in most wine shops. These little things are basically jewelry for your wineglass. If you're like me, though, you'll likely forget whether you're the decorative bunch of grapes or the decorative wedge of Brie piece in about five minutes (or five sips of merlot). Small colored rubber bands are cheaper, and you can write each guest's name on them with a pen.

A Different Kind of Fish Story

When making a cake, decorations are more than a minor detail; they're the crowning glory of your party (just like a Southern girl's hair). If you know what you're doing, that is. I made my daughter's wedding cake, so I figured a birthday cake for my father-in-law should be a no-brainer. Well, I learned that you should never be overconfident.

My father-in-law loved to fish, so I planned to let him go fishing at his party with a complete fishing scene. I used the same recipe that I had used for the wedding cake—sour cream cocoa. The first cake didn't rise. It tasted like a brownie, though, so I figured I could use it to decorate. I made a second sheet cake, and it turned out perfectly. I set the short-but-delicious cake next to it. The taller cake (frosted in green) would serve as the bank, the inadvertent brownie (frosted in blue) as the water. I dyed some coconut brown to serve as seaweed. It looked like you'd expect brown coconut to look—a bad idea! The color was atrocious. I had some fish-shaped cheddar crackers on hand, so I put a few in the water. They looked all right but did nothing for the taste of the cake. It was getting late enough that I couldn't remedy my design, so I headed off to the party.

I remembered that we didn't have candles, so I stopped off on the way. Candles that would not blow out were the latest rage, so I figured they'd help the joke of a cake. Even that didn't work out. Some friends had given my father-in-law a cake with these candles the night before.

I figured that I couldn't win with this cake, but that's not quite true! My father-in-law, who is now ninety-five, remembers that cake fondly. In fact, it's probably the thing he remembers most about me. Being a gentleman, though, he also reminds me of the lovely cakes I have made over the years. The cake was a fiasco, but we're still sharing a laugh even now!

—Joyce Duncan
Cartersville, Georgia

When it comes to your food, details are just as important. That Thanksgiving turkey just wouldn't be the same if it weren't nestled on a bed of parsley. Those little canapés wouldn't look as nice without the little dab of caviar or chives. You might think that you're saving time by skimping out on the details, but don't. A bit of decoration on your food is an inexpensive way to make even the simplest dish look spectacular. In fact, sugar, I'll let you in on a little secret—putting the time into the details lets you skimp on other things! You might make a plain old pot roast in the Crock-Pot, but sprinkle some fresh herbs on top, and it looks

Deborah Ford's "Retaining 39" Party

When I throw a party, everything is in the details. When I was thirty-eight, I had to wear braces. Braces are bad enough at any age, but with wrinkles (or "laugh lines," as I like to think of them), they're far worse. I made a deal with my orthodontist—the braces had to be off by my fortieth birthday, or I wouldn't wear them. I had a big "retaining thirty-nine" party planned, and there wasn't going to be any heavy metal there. He took the braces off the day before my party. I gave everyone in my orthodontist's office a T-shirt that said WE HELPED STRAIGHTEN DEBORAH OUT! *For all my other guests, I gave T-shirts that said* HEAVY METAL NO MORE. *For centerpieces, I used birthday cards I saved over the years, along with the funniest cards I could find for all ages, and we all had fun reading them. Everyone had such a good time, I'm on my twelfth thirty-ninth birthday party and loving it. When the time comes to throw my fiftieth birthday party (twenty or thirty years from now), I'll have a FLASHing party—because fifty-ish ladies are so HOT!!!*

A PEARL GIRL KNOWS

At High-Falutin' milestone events (weddings, anniversary parties, retirement banquets), place a small disposable camera on each table so that guests can capture the memories. Place a basket (decorated in ribbons to match the event's colors) by the door labeled PLEASE DEPOSIT CAMERAS HERE.

Goodness Gracious!

Canapé is the French word for "couch," and the English word for any toast or cracker with a fancy little topping, such as cheese or anchovies. So next time you think you're hungry enough to eat the furniture, reach for a canapé!

good enough for company. If you're really at a loss, you might just buy a preroasted chicken from the grocery store deli but surround it with thinly sliced pieces of lemon, and suddenly you've got a gourmet meal.

Whiskey River . . . Keeping Everyone Afloat

An empty glass kills a party fast! Stock up your bar in advance (liquor doesn't wilt), and once your guests walk in the door, offer them a drink. Always have a nonalcoholic choice, or, better yet, offer a special nonalcoholic cocktail. (A simple combination of cranberry and grapefruit juices topped off with club soda looks and tastes interesting without requiring

All Dolled Up for a Southern Party

I was reading the good book one night, when Hebrews 12:12–13 struck me: "So take a new grip with your tired hands. Stand firm on your shaky legs and mark out a straight path for your feet so that those who follow you though weak and lame will not fall or hurt themselves, but become strong." We Southern girls needed to look back on our lives and find someone who stood strong, and did the best they good to keep traditions alive, even through hard times.

With the help of my friends, I sent out invitations with pictures of old dolls. Our invitations said that each lady was special, and she should bring an old doll and a story of a special Southern woman. We decorated the tables in white cloths, with pink, green, and white dishes. We placed a silver tea pitcher on each table filled with magnolia and gardenia leaves. And, of course, we used white cloth napkins. We decorated a special table with old pearls, white gloves, kerosene lamps, flowers, and my grandmother's fur stole, but the decoration was not complete until the guests arrived and set down their dolls in the middle.

During dessert, we discussed how we dreamed our lives would be when we were young and playing with dolls. But through the influence of others and of God, we all succeeded and held traditions alive for our families to follow. We discussed ladies who inspired us such as Queen, who was the grandmother of Alex Haley, and Helen Keller. The party was very special—old dolls like us need to get together sometimes to honor those who came before, and to pave the way for those who come after.

—Ann Hayes
   Florence, Alabama

any special preparation.) Some people do not drink for health or religious reasons, and no Pearl Girl worth her salt would want to think that she was the reason they fell off the wagon!

A PEARL GIRL KNOWS

Most of us know at least one former alcoholic who no longer imbibes but who wants to socialize at parties where alcohol is served. Try not to single him out. Pour him a nonaloholic cocktail, and when serving wine, skip past his seat without saying anything. If you believe that he will feel singled out as the only nondrinker, keep him company by skipping the alcohol yourself.

For a High-Falutin' party, it is best to have at least one professional bartender. (There's also nothing wrong with dressing up one of your friends—preferably one whose idea of a mixed drink goes beyond an extra shake to the beer can—to save a bit of money.) If you have more than fifty people at your party, you will need more than one bartender: start with at least one for parties under fifty, and add another bartender for each additional fifty guests expected. If the budget is an issue, a morning event is preferable. For morning events you can get by with no alcohol or less potent "morning cocktails" such as mimosas and Bloody Marys. For any evening High-Falutin' party, a full, open bar is the best choice, but if you are on a limited budget, an open bar with a limited selection—such as just wine, beer, and soda—is acceptable. Whatever you do, avoid a cash bar. Cash changing hands at a party is as tacky as wearing white after Labor Day.

For a Falutin' party, it's fine to tend bar yourself (or better yet, rope an available man into the job for you). In fact, if you have a friend or family member who is a little awkward at parties, he'll be grateful to have a job that can be fun, and will give him something to talk about. "What's in a Long Island iced tea?" can always get a conversation started if nothing else can. (Be warned, though—after he tastes a couple of what he's pouring, your shy little bartender might not be able to shut up.)

For a Just Falutin' Around party, your guests will expect to serve themselves (though they'll be more than happy to have your pretty little hands mixing up their cocktails). Set out beer and white wine on ice, red wine, liquor (if you desire) and mixers on a table, and let the fun begin!

SOUTHERN TRANSLATION

sippin' whiskey [sip´ ən] **n.** *the best-quality bourbon—ladies sip it slowly.*
homebrew [hōm´ broō] **n.** *liquor made behind the shed—ladies avoid it at all costs.*

You'll need to stock your bar well in advance of your party. For quantities, some party planners say that you should plan on two drinks per person. These party planners don't know my friends! For a cocktail party, I plan on around four drinks per person. For wine with dinner, I plan on at least half a bottle per person. If we don't finish the alcohol, I figure that we can always use it at the next party. It's tricky to figure how much you need, and I like to overbuy rather than underbuy. There are a couple of rules of thumb that help: If there will be more women than men, I stock up on wine; if more men, I stock up on beer. For parties with younger people, vodka is usually the liquor of choice, but older folks often prefer bourbon, rum, or scotch. When planning quantities, remember that ice is no minor detail. Always plan to have too much. For the drinks themselves, plan at least one pound per person; for chilling the drinks, plan on another pound per person. An ice company or beverage supply company will have ice available in quantities. Bring coolers in the car with you (and borrow coolers from friends and family if you do not have enough).

Well-Stocked Bar for an All-Out Party

❑ **Liquor**: *blended whiskey, bourbon, dark and light rum, gin, scotch, vodka*

❑ **Liqueurs**: *amaretto, crème de menthe, Kahlúa, and Cointreau, Grand Marnier, or triple sec*

❑ **Wine**: *dry and sweet vermouth, sherry, champagne, and red and white wines*

❑ **Beer**: *domestic, imported, and light*

❑ **Mixers**: *club soda, cranberry, ginger ale, orange juice, Coke (diet and regular), lemon soda, tomato juice, and tonic*

❑ **Garnishes**: *lemons, limes, maraschino cherries, and olives*

❑ **Bar stuff**: *corkscrew, bottle openers, long spoon, water pitcher, knife, cloths, ice, napkins, ice bucket, and a bartending book to figure out what in the world to do with all that stuff!*

For a Falutin' or Just Falutin' Around Party, a bar will be extra special if you mix up at least one "specialty of the house" drink. (At a High-Falutin' Party, it's great if the bartender has a specialty drink to mix in individual portions, such as mojitos—just make sure you have enough bartenders, as these drinks take extra time.) A good punch or a pitcher of something special is more interesting than a couple of bottles of white wine. And please remember to have at

This recipe was supplied by the good folks at Tope Là (meaning "clasping of hands"), a restaurant in Hammond, Louisiana, honoring Louisiana's French and American heritage.

> 4 tea bags
> 2 cups hot water
> 2 cups sugar
> 2 to 3 cups bourbon, gin, vodka, or rum (just one, sugah!)
> 1 12-ounce can frozen lemonade, thawed
> 1 12-ounce can frozen orange juice, thawed

Steep the tea bags in the hot water for 3 to 4 minutes. Remove the bags, and add sugar. Stir the liquid until the sugar is dissolved. Mix in the remaining ingredients, and freeze. Remove from the freezer 30 minutes before serving, stir, and serve. (The drinks will be slushy.)

least one nonalcoholic choice—it should be just as special as the hard stuff.

Goodness Gracious!

The Hurricane, a potent, deep red rum-based drink, means Mardi Gras to many—and hangovers to many more. Legend has it that bartender Pat O'Brien invented the drink in the 1940s to get rid of bottles of rum that his distributors had been unloading. He poured the drink into a hurricane lamp–shaped glass and gave it away to sailors. Whatever the drink's origins, it really sneaks up on you, so take it easy on the Hurricanes when you visit the Big Easy.

Sangria

2 bottles dry red wine
1 cup cognac
½ cup orange liqueur (triple sec or Cointreau)
¼ cup granulated sugar (superfine is best)
1 orange, sliced thin
1 lemon, sliced thin
1 apple, cored and cut into chunks
2 cups seltzer

Combine the wine, cognac, orange liqueur, and sugar. Stir until the sugar is dissolved. Add the fruit, and chill for at least 1 hour. Pour the drink mixture into punch bowl, stir in the seltzer, and add a couple of handfuls of ice cubes.

Iced Tea Punch

4 cups boiling water
4 family-size tea bags
4 regular bags mint tea
1 6-ounce can frozen lemonade, thawed
½ cup sugar
5 cups cold water

Pour boiling water into a large pitcher over both kinds of tea bags. Let the tea sit 3 to 4 minutes; then remove the tea bags. Stir in the lemonade and sugar until dissolved. Chill the mixture until cool. Pour it into a punch bowl, and dilute with 5 cups cold water (or more or less, depending on your taste) and several generous handfuls of ice.

Baptist Cocktail

This may not be your mother's Baptist Cocktail. Dozens of completely different drinks with the same name have been floating around the South for at least as long as I've been drinking. (Whoops! I mean sipping.) The only things that they have in common: they're nonalcoholic, and they're delicious.

    6 cups pineapple juice
    1 6-ounce can frozen limeade, thawed
    2 2-liter bottles ginger ale

Mix all the ingredients in a large pitcher, chill, and add to a punch bowl with ice. Sometimes (especially when the punch is for children) scoops of lime sherbet are floated on the top.

Hey Good Lookin', What You Got Cooking ...
Food and Service

Pearl Girls don't feel comfortable entertaining unless they offer something to eat to their guests. It may be nothing more than an emergency box of cookies kept for drop-in guests, or it may be an elaborate buffet for a fancy dress ball, but Southern ladies love to feed and pamper. Weeks of care and preparation go into the entertaining menu, and the same care should go into the service.

SOUTHERN TRANSLATION

family style [fam´ ə lē stīl] **adj.** *each item is placed in a serving dish and passed around the table—guests serve themselves.*

buffet style [bə fā´ stīl] **adj.** *food is placed on a separate sideboard or table—guests serve themselves and bring the food back to their seats.*

plate style [plāt´ stīl] **adj.** *food is plated on the kitchen and served to guests at their seats.*

French style [french´ stīl] **adj.** *each guest is seated before an empty plate—food is brought on platters to the diners and served by a butler or waiter to each guest.*

For a High-Falutin' seated meal, French service is considered the most elegant. A waiter or butler brings a platter of food to the guest, the guest selects his portion, and the waiter serves. This type of service is time-consuming and very expensive. (Professional butlers recommend at least one server to each six diners.) It is also so uncommon that it may confuse guests, who may not know what to do when a big old rack of lamb is suddenly in their faces. Because this method of serving is so uncommon and may make guests feel uncomfortable, I would not recommend it even for a High-Falutin' event.

More common (and less expensive) is plate service. Plates are arranged in the kitchen and brought out to each guest. This method of service is what you will see in all the best American restaurants. For a seated High-Falutin' event, plate service is the best bet, though there's nothing wrong with a buffet, as long as it is elegantly presented. If you want to spend a bit more of your (or Daddy's) money, "hand service" involves one waiter for every two guests. Food is brought out by the waiters, who stand behind the guest, and each guest is served simultaneously. This method is dramatic, but because it involves so many waiters, it will cost a lot of money.

Goodness Gracious!

In the 1950s, plate service was uncommon and considered rather tacky in European restaurants. Guests expected to be served by trained waiters, and they wanted a large selection. Today, American-style plate service is the norm even in the snootiest French restaurants.

To serve plate style, set down food from the left and remove from the right. Serve beverages from the right (unless you have a left-handed guest who has moved his glass). For a High-Falutin' event, it is better to have a professional server (or to rope in a friend or family member to help you). If the hostess is serving, she will not have time to tend to her guests. In fact, even for a Falutin' or Just Falutin' Around event, serving your guests will require you to be up and away from your table, so you won't be part of the conversation. Your guests would much prefer your pretty smile at the table to having you run back and forth to the kitchen.

One thing a cook can do for dramatic effect is to finish a dish tableside. Fruit flambé or baked Alaska can be finished next to the table (dim the lights for best effect), or a salad can be mixed on a cart. Paying your waitstaff to do this can be the highlight of a High-Falutin' meal, but it's a great way to add something memorable to a Falutin' meal if you do it yourself. Even if you serve the rest of the dinner buffet style, having a dramatic dessert service can make the evening.

A PEARL GIRL KNOWS

Always remember to tip for good service. Remember, their trailer costs as much as yours (and possibly more).

For most Falutin' or Just Falutin' Around events, I recommend buffet service (nothing to do with Jimmy Buffet). Family service (sitting down together and passing around plates) is common, but there's always some person at the end of the table who forgets to pass, and it is the hostess's responsibility to say, for the fourth time, "Bubba, honey, would you mind passing on those platters that are gathering around your place?" Family service also leads to a cluttered table, and it doesn't leave you room to showcase your beautiful centerpiece. Buffet service is also nice for a High-Falutin' event that doesn't involve a seated dinner—an hors d'oeuvre or dessert buffet is elegant at even the most High-Falutin' event.

Lay out your buffet elegantly. Set out each course sequentially—salads at the beginning of the buffet, main and side dishes in the middle, and desserts at the end or, better yet, if you have the room, set each course on a separate table. In traditional European service, salads are served after the main course, to refresh diners. This is not standard in America, however. Besides, in the South "salad" can mean anything from macaroni to Jell-O, so the logic does not apply. Down here, it's better to keep your salad at the beginning of your buffet. An attended buffet involves a waiter or chef standing behind the table and serving each guest, and if you decide to have a High-Falutin' party with buffet service, it is probably the way to go. (At the very least, have one attended station, such as a roast-carving area, and let the rest

Goodness Gracious!

If your husband takes pride in carving up the Thanksgiving turkey, he's just showing his (upper) class. Along with the expected Latin and religious teaching, carving meat, poultry, and game were once considered an important part of any nobleman's education.

of the buffet be self-service.) Attended buffets are more elegant, but, of course, cost more money. You can, of course, plan to serve behind the buffet yourself, but don't think you'll be sitting with your guests if you do so. Most likely, fast eaters will be up again for seconds before you sit down to eat your firsts.

When laying out your buffet, place beverages and silverware at the end of the table (unless you have already laid them out on the dining table). To make things easier for your guests, wrap individual sets of silverware in a napkin. It will be easier to carry back to the table, and your guests have only one thing to pick up. Even if beverages are going to be on the end of the buffet, it is always a good idea to keep a couple of carafes of water on the table so that guests can refill their glasses during the meal.

Tips, Touches, Techniques, and Tradition

When dinner is served at a High-Falutin' or Falutin' party, you will need to make a seating arrangement. Back when our grandmothers were serving dinners, they'd pull out their (immaculately styled) hair over where to seat people. They had to alternate men and women and separate couples, but they also had to figure out who was the most important, and seat people accordingly. I say, Forget that, honey! Every guest, whether he's a general contractor or the guy pounding the nails, is equally important. When you do your seating chart, I think that it's great to honor tradition. Tradition is what we Pearl Girls are about. Splitting up couples keeps them from chatting together all night, and alternating men and women keeps the conversation lively (no endless baseball trivia at one end of the table and talk of diets at the other). But social precedence has as much place in party planning as a mangy dog in the parlor—throw it out and good riddance. If there's a guest of honor, you might want to seat him next to you. Otherwise, try to seat people according to their interests. (If you slyly put the single people across from each other, Miss Matchmaker, that's your business.) Seating people this way is common sense combined with a healthy respect for tradition—the Pearl Girls way.

Goodness Gracious!

In the United States, the head of the table is the position of honor, but in France, honored guests are seated in the middle.

At a High-Falutin or Falutin' party, place cards are a great way for people to know where to sit, and it helps them to avoid the embarrassment of asking their neighbor's name for the third time that night. For a High-Falutin' party, the place card should be a simple cream or white card with the guest's name written by hand in ink or engraved.

For a Falutin' party, the simple place card will look elegant, and will always be appropriate. But why serve your guests plain old meat loaf if you've got filet mignon hidden in the icebox? Draw a picture, or cut a photo out of a magazine, to show something interesting for each guest. That NASCAR fan might have a car on his place card. The woman who studied cooking in France a bottle of wine and some cheese on hers. And the lawyer might have a tiny devil (and dollar signs, of course) on his.

As a finishing touch, consider printing or writing the menu for each guest to take home. Not only will you not have to tell your guests for the twelfth time what's in the gratin, they'll appreciate your pulling out the red carpet for them.

Freezer Pleasers . . . Icebox Cuisine

When I entertain, I like to prepare as much as possible ahead of time. Some Southern gals are part Julia Child, part Martha Stewart, part Jacqueline Kennedy Onassis. . . . I'm none of the above. (None of them are Southern girls, sugah.) I like to please my family and friends with well-made dishes that taste delicious, but I'm too busy to spend hours in the kitchen.

A PEARL GIRL KNOWS

The freezer is a perfect place to keep your brushes during half-finished painting projects. Just wrap the bristles in aluminum foil, freeze, and when you're ready to paint, thaw and use. That's a freezer pleaser to me!

You can spend the morning of your party whipping up a béarnaise sauce, or you can spend it whipping up the perfect outfit. As for me, I'd rather have good food *and* look good for my guests. The way to do it is to make as much ahead as possible. Dishes that you can freeze days before the party can impress your guests like you've worked like Cinderella, but still let you have time to look like you've had a little help from your fairy godmother.

Appetizer

Almost anything made of phyllo or puff pastry—cheese bundles, spinach pies, olive twists—freezes beautifully for up to one month.

Sausage Pinwheels

1 package frozen puff pastry (two sheets)
1 roll of country sausage
Optional ingredients: 1 sprinkle of red pepper flakes, ¼ cup chopped green onions, fresh or dried sage, ¼ cup hard, grated cheese

Allow the puff pastry to thaw for about half an hour, and unroll both sheets. Spread half of the sausage mixed with any optional ingredients on each sheet, then roll up from the long end of the pastry jelly-roll fashion to form a long, thin log. Wrap the log in one layer of plastic wrap and then one layer of aluminum foil. When you are ready to cook, heat oven to 400 degrees F, unwrap and slice the roll into ½-inch slices, and bake for 15 to 20 minutes, until done.

Soup

God bless the Cuisinart. If you keep frozen pureed vegetables in the freezer, soups or sauces take seconds to make. Winter squashes, carrots, and sweet potatoes make beautiful frozen purees, but experiment with other vegetables for more interesting soups.

Butternut Squash Soup

1 butternut squash
2 cans chicken broth or 4 cups stock
Salt and pepper, to taste
Optional garnishes: croutons, sliced green onions, minced chives, a
    dollop of goat cheese, a sprinkle of paprika, sliced fully cooked
    chorizo or summer sausage

Preheat the oven to 375 degrees F. Slice the squash in half, and lay it cut-side down on a foil-lined baking sheet. (The foil makes cleanup easy.) Bake until the squash is soft, 40 minutes to more than an hour depending on the squash. Let it sit until cool enough to handle. Scoop out the seeds and discard them. Scoop the flesh into a food processor or blender, and blend until smooth. Freeze the puree in a Ziploc bag, plastic-covered container, or in ice cube trays.

When you're ready to eat, place the squash puree in a pot. (It isn't necessary to defrost.) Add the chicken broth. Cook the mixture over a medium flame until warm. Taste and add salt and pepper if desired. If the soup is too thick, add a little water to thin it, and adjust your seasonings. Garnish your soup with any of the optional garnishes, if desired.

Salad

Normally, a make-ahead green salad is nothing but a soggy mess, and a frozen salad is something so silly, only a man would try it. This salad can and should be made twenty-four hours ahead and kept in the refrigerator.

24-Hour Salad

6 cups chopped lettuce
Salt, pepper, and sugar to taste
3 hard-boiled eggs, sliced
10-ounce package frozen green peas, thawed
16 ounces bacon, fried and crumbled (or 1 package already-cooked bacon)
8 ounces shredded Swiss cheese
⅓ cup sliced green onion
1 cup mayonnaise
Paprika

Place 3 cups of the lettuce in a bowl, and sprinkle it with salt, pepper, and sugar. Lay the sliced eggs on top, and sprinkle them with more salt. Layer the peas, remaining lettuce, bacon, cheese, and green onion (reserving a few for the top), and spread with mayonnaise. Cover and chill for twenty-four hours. Sprinkle the salad with reserved onions and paprika.

—Joy Fauver Haglund
Deerfield Beach, Florida

Most casseroles, stews, chilies, or meat loaves freeze beautifully. If you think that a casserole is déclassé, call it something different! Lasagna and moussaka are nothing but casseroles, but they sound so good that no one would turn their nose up at them. Rename your Aunt Edna's "Chicken and Green Bean Casserole Surprise" as "Poulet et Haricot," and you're looking like a culinary genius.

Ropa Vieja

Latin flavors have become part of life in the United States. Ropa Vieja means "old clothes" in Spanish (probably because it looks a little like your husband's old flannel shirt before you "accidentally" sent it out to the Goodwill). It is a Latin treat popular in South Florida.

1 beef flank steak (1½ to 2 pounds)
2 onions, one chopped and one sliced
1 bay leaf
Salt and pepper, to taste
2 tablespoons olive oil
3 bell peppers (preferably 1 green, 1 yellow, 1 red), cut into strips
4 cloves garlic, finely minced
2 jalapeno peppers, seeded and minced
¼ teaspoon cinnamon
1 small can (about 16 ounces) crushed tomatoes

Chop the steak into 4 large chunks. In a large pot, heat the meat, chopped onion, bay leaf, some salt, and 5 cups of water to a boil. Reduce heat, cover, and simmer until the meat is tender (roughly 3 hours). Remove the pot from the heat and let it stand about half an hour. Remove the meat, and shred it with a fork. Reserve 2 cups of broth, and discard the rest of the juice. In a skillet, heat the oil over a medium flame. Add the sliced onion, bell peppers, garlic, and a pinch of salt. Cook until the vegetables are tender but not brown. Add the hot peppers and cinnamon, and cook for a few seconds. Add the tomatoes. Cook for a few minutes. Add the reserved broth and beef. Cook about 10 minutes. Taste for seasoning, and add salt and pepper as needed. Cool the dish and place in plastic container, cover, and freeze. When you're ready to eat, reheat the meat in a microwave, or defrost and heat on the stove. Ropa Vieja is traditionally served with hot white rice.

A PEARL GIRL KNOWS

The best way to thaw a turkey . . . blow in his ear.

Dessert

Anything from ice cream to an icebox pie freezes beautifully and, if your guests are stuffed, can wait until they clear a little room for dessert.

Oreo Pie

22 Oreo cookies, crushed
⅓ cup butter (melted)
½ gallon vanilla ice cream, softened (substitute pistachio, mint, or coffee
    for a change of flavor)
16-ounce tub Cool Whip
1 bottle fudge ice cream topping (small bottle, or about 1½ cups)

Reserve a handful of Oreos. Mix the rest of the Oreos with the melted butter, and press them into a 9-by-13-inch pan. Press the softened ice cream on top. Spread with the fudge topping, and cover with the Cool Whip. Sprinkle the pie with the reserved Oreos. Freeze your dessert until ready to serve.

—Joy Fauver Haglund (with thanks to her sister, Coni Marble)
  Deerfield Beach, Florida

Frozen Lemon Pie

½ of a large box gingersnaps
6 tablespoons butter
6-ounce can frozen lemonade, defrosted for a couple of hours in the fridge
8 ounces Cool Whip
1 can (14 ounces) sweetened condensed milk

Process the gingersnaps in a food processor, or break them up by placing them in a Ziploc bag and hitting it with a rolling pin. Measure out 1½ cups crushed gingersnaps, and save the rest of crumbs for another use. Mix the butter and gingersnaps, and press them into a pie plate. Bake for 8 to 10 minutes, and cool. If desired, a ready-made graham cracker crust can be used instead. (Just open up and use.) Mix the lemonade, Cool Whip, and milk in a medium bowl. Pour the filling into the shell and freeze until ready to use. You'll have slightly more filling than will fit in the shell—if you'd like, you can use the filling recipe for two shells, freeze, and when you're ready to serve, arrange fresh berries to fill the two pies.

Famine, Flood, and Fire . . .
Planning for Disaster

If you've planned well and stocked up your house correctly, nothing should go wrong at a party . . . in the world of women's magazines and cooking shows, that is. Here in the real world, the rice will boil over, the wax will drip on the table, big Bubba Johnson will pass out in the parlor, and the dog will bite the guest of honor. Disasters will happen, and the best that we can do is plan for them.

SOUTHERN TRANSLATION

afar [ə far´] n. *a place that is not near; your guest's hair when he does a drunken Polynesian fire dance.*

One of the most obvious things a hostess needs to do (and one of the things we rarely take the time to do between shuttling the kids to soccer practice and finishing our filing at work) is to sit down and think about what might go wrong. If it's Alabama in July, that beautiful swan ice sculpture will melt—we need a catch basin. If we're serving alcohol, guests will throw back one too many—we need to arrange towels for sloppy drinks and transportation for sloppy guests. If we're using a chafing dish, we need extra Sterno and a fire extinguisher. A little planning ahead can eliminate running around like a headless chicken when there's red wine on the living room rug and a suspicious dog in the upstairs toilet.

Bats in the Belfry

When I was in college, a Pearl Girl friend of mine got me a job hostessing at the High Point Furniture Mart in North Carolina. We worked in a big, barnlike space that the furniture company used only twice a year for big shows. The rest of the year, the space stood empty (or mostly empty, as we found out). We would dress in our best and welcome buyers to the showroom for various parties. All the parties took place during the day, but the press party took place in the evening.

My friend and I slipped on our little black dresses and our pearls and went to meet the magazine editors. The sales reps showed up at five and drank steadily until the editors showed up an hour and a half later, but my friend and I wanted to keep cool, ladylike heads, so we stayed away from the alcohol.

The editors showed up and started chatting with the sales reps. Then, from the corner of the room, there was a shriek. A hysterical magazine editor ran out as fast as her little legs could carry her. Then, from another corner, another scream. Soon, the room was in a melee, and my friend and I saw what was wrong. A family of bats had taken up residence in the rafters and was dive-bombing the party!

The editors fled as the sales reps, hooting and hollering and a little too tipsy to come close to actually hitting anything but the table lamps, tried to use everything from throw pillows to walking canes to corral the bats. Realizing that the sales reps were having too much fun chasing the bats to tend to the press, my friend and I grabbed some press kits and ran out to catch the editors before they fled.

The editors were shaken, the sales reps had a few bumps and bruises (not from the bats—from falling all over each other and the furniture), and the bats soon found the windows and ended their kamikaze adventure unhurt. Even though it may not have been the best party ever, I think we actually made more sales than we would have otherwise—those editors sure had a memorable evening. It goes to show that if you keep a cool head, you can rescue any party, even if you've got bats in the belfry!

—Aimee Weaver
Dunwoody, Georgia

No matter how wonderful your party is, little folks get tired of us old people and our boring old stories. I know that you've brought your own little Pearl Girls and boys up right, and they'd never streak naked through the living room or set the buffet table on fire (or at least you're crossing your fingers that they won't do it in front of the guests), but idle little hands will get into mischief. Keeping children entertained (or at least occupied) helps to stop disaster before it happens. If you can, set aside a room stocked with videos, board games and books, sugary treats, and a teenage girl to supervise. (She's probably as bored as the little folks.) For a meal, there's a reason the children's table is an honored tradition—the kids can eat the foods that they like, make faces (and noises)

Striking Back When Disaster Strikes— What to Have on Hand

- ☐ Extra towels and garbage bags.
- ☐ Fire extinguisher.
- ☐ Spot remover, club soda, vinegar, and baking soda for various spills, stains, and sloppiness.
- ☐ First-aid kit.
- ☐ Rock salt for steps and driveways (especially if you're a Southern gal trapped in the North or Midwest).
- ☐ Extra fuses.
- ☐ Extra ice, glasses, and alcohol.
- ☐ Toilet plunger and rubber gloves (and a male to do the dirty work).
- ☐ List of local cab companies.
- ☐ List of emergency numbers (including the pizza man's for when the roast burns).
- ☐ A chauffeur (or a friend dressed to the nines) on call for drunken guests.
- ☐ When all else fails—a bottle of wine and some earplugs.

at each other, and leave whenever they're finished (and we don't have to watch Kayla dribble sweet potatoes down her chin and hear Chase burping the alphabet).

Don't Forget the Guest of Honor!

The week before a party is the time when you lay the groundwork so that you can take it easy the day of the party. It's about planning, and it's about preparation . . . but don't forget to take time for a little pampering. So get those lists in order, polish up that silver, make your cakes and casseroles, and stock up that bar, but when you're done, chase the kids out of the house (or plop them in front of a video—it's not a sin every once in a while), draw a hot bath, put on your favorite CD, light a few candles, and celebrate the best Pearl Girl you know—you!

Fitting Together the Pieces—
Family Get-togethers

At family get-togethers in the South, we bring together all the mismatched pieces—some warped, some bent, some out of place, but all belonging—of the crazy puzzle that is the Southern family. Somehow we fit together (or at least have fits together). We renew our bonds—and ourselves—by taking time for our loved ones. There was a time when aunts, uncles, and grandparents were part of our everyday lives. Today, this is not necessarily true, but a family reunion is one way of recapturing some of the nurturing and warmth felt long ago.

My daddy died when I was ten years old. I cannot remember any scheduled family get-togethers, maybe because Mother was too busy making ends meet seven days a week, or maybe because no one took charge to make things happen. In fact, I never saw much of Daddy's family, maybe because my cousins were (at least according to my mother) not a good influence.

I clearly remember my first family reunion. My first "bless his heart," a term I use for all the ex-men in my life since I had to bless those poor dears so many times, had a very large family, and there was never a Sunday afternoon when his grandparents' home was not filled with family and friends. From every week's Sunday supper to the biggest to-do on holidays, the home was the same: two big dining tables full of food, dessert in the kitchen, and sweet tea, lemonade, and ice water on the back porch. I had never had a real reunion with my own family, and now I was having one every single week with his.

My next "bless his heart" also had a close family, and his mother made sure her two boys and their families got together for her Sunday morning breakfast of silver-dollar pancakes. She would play with her grandchildren, spending hours cooking, reading, dressing up, fixing hair, baking her famous bread, and just being there when they were sick.

My third "bless his heart" was part of a wonderful Jewish family. He was blessed with a beautiful daughter, and I just fell in love with her. I helped plan her bat mitzvah with her extended family, and I have to say I learned from the best about how to entertain.

All my sweethearts' families celebrated often, but differently. Southerners have different ways of celebrating with their families, and even within our own families, we're a jumble, but somehow we all manage to fit together.

Beyond the Chicken Dance— Family Reunion Activities

- Challenge everyone to a "family trivia" game—where did Aunt and Uncle McLeod get married, what was Grandpa's first job, which Armstrong boy made varsity baseball? As long as you don't bring up any of Jimmy's five DUIs, everyone will have fun and learn about their family.
- Drag out the horseshoes, croquet set, and shuffleboard for an old-fashioned games tournament.
- Hang doughnuts from a string. The first to eat the doughnut (no hands, please) without dropping any wins. (This one is probably best left to the kids.)
- Play "match the baby." Have a table full of baby pictures, with a number next to each one. Whoever matches the most pictures to names wins.
- Tug of war, three-legged race, and red rover make great games when everyone is hepped up on too much pecan pie and lemonade. For these physical games, just make sure the little children are pretty evenly matched for size.

Homecomings, clan meetings, pig roasts, weddings, reunions, funerals, tailgating for the big game, fishing tournaments, birthdays, anniversaries, baby showers, hunting parties, quilting, canning, Easter, Christmas, Fourth of July, Thanksgiving, and just rocking on the front porch . . . Southern families get together for any and all reasons.

If you want to plan a reunion, June to August are the best months (so the little ones won't be at school). There are numerous books to help you plan a reunion. It can be as simple as a backyard barbecue or as elaborate as a catered banquet. Whatever you choose, the important thing is getting together as a family.

Fifty Years Flew By in the Blink of an Eye

(excerpted from the syndicated column,
"Sweet Tea and Sour Notes")

With the help of many loving friends and family members, my brother and I are planning the fiftieth anniversary celebration of our parents' marriage. It seems most of the other people who have such celebrations are old, but my parents aren't. They are still relatively the same age as when I was born, married and had children. Through my eyes and in my mind, they just don't age. That state of denial also works well for me and my brother. If our parents don't age, we stay pretty young, as well.

But the dates written in the Bible tell the truth. And the truth is this year, John Ray and Lottye Betts Beasley, parents of Rick Beasley and Eva Ann Dorris, will have been married fifty years. They say time truly flies when you are having fun.

I remember the warm and funny stories of the early years when money was scarce—the years Daddy calls their "hat in hand years" of asking for credit to start businesses, build a home and buy the farm that would become our home, our safe haven and the family's gathering place. The home where daily a child or grandchild stops by to visit, borrow tools, tractors and four-wheelers, checks to see what's fresh in the garden or hopes to catch just a few moments of peace and quiet amid the lawn chairs and large cedar trees.

I remember so well our walks at the end of the long summer days. Mother and Daddy would walk down the road to check the cows or the garden. They would hold hands while I ran ahead, chasing fireflies, racing the dogs or circling them on my bicycle. The good-night kisses were distributed from their bedroom each night after a few precious moments of snuggling between them.

Even as a child, I knew I was blessed. I knew not everyone had the kind of loving home I was fortunate enough to return to each day. During my school-age years, Daddy would ask every evening how things were going and "do I need to go down there and straighten anyone out?" I never asked him to go and straightening out would have been done in a civil parent/teacher conference, but I knew they were there. If I met a battle I couldn't win, I knew where the reinforcements were.

These days, as we spend hours poring over photo albums and scouring address books for old and new friends to add to the invitation list, we admit the only real fault we can find with the two strong individuals fifty years into a long honeymoon is that through all these years they've made it look so easy—much easier than we as adults have discovered it is.

They made being friends, parents, providers and role models look so easy and so natural. Once we walked in their shoes, we realized there was nothing easy about it. They are just such a complementary team with the same ideals that they draw their strength from each other.

Fifty years is a long time. For John Ray and Lottye Betts, it isn't nearly long enough.

Happy anniversary, Mom and Dad. I love you.

—Eva Ann Dorris
   Pontotoc, Mississippi

CHAPTER 6

Leaving It to the Last Minute

"Remember, Heather, the last four letters of the word American are 'I can.' "
—HEATHER WHITESTONE
   ALABAMA GIRL AND FORMER MISS AMERICA,
   REMEMBERING THE WORDS OF HER MOTHER

I am still determined to be cheerful and happy, in whatever situation I may be; for I have learned from experience that the greater part of our happiness or misery depends upon our disposition, and not upon our circumstances.
—MARTHA WASHINGTON
   NEW KENT COUNTY, VIRGINIA

SINCE YOU'RE A REAL PEARL GIRL, YOU KNOW HOW IM-
portant it is to begin planning your party weeks (or
sometimes months) ahead. Sometimes, though, your
child shows up with a Swedish foreign exchange student and
announces that if you don't throw him a wedding next week,
he's going to Las Vegas. Maybe your husband is getting an
unexpected promotion, maybe your in-laws just parked their
RV in your driveway, maybe you forgot your best friend's
birthday . . . whatever the reason, sometimes you have to entertain guests unexpectedly.

A PEARL GIRL KNOWS

*To throw the best last-minute parties, be "party ready" all year.
Stock up on baking supplies, nonperishable food, wine and liquor,
and small gifts.*

You and I both know that these days, you can call the
grocery store the day before a party, order a shrimp platter, a
plate of veggies and dip, and a cake. We've all been to parties
where the only preparation is a quick call and a drive to the
store. There's nothing wrong with doing it this way, and I've

done it myself when time is short. But Pearl Girls want to put their special touch on every party, even one we throw at the last minute. We might have to cut corners, we might have to cheat a bit, and we might have to hide some messy socks and messy kids, but we want our parties—even those we're throwing because our son, together with his entire fraternity, showed up at the last minute—to have our own special touch.

When to Throw It Together at the Last Minute, and When to Throw in the Towel

Unless you have an unlimited budget and a lot of connections, it is difficult to impossible to throw a High-Falutin' affair at the last minute. Getting invitations printed and sent out, securing caterers and florists, and preparing an elegant meal in just a few days are beyond the abilities of most hostesses and checkbooks. We love dressing up like the beauty queens we are and putting on the grits, but when we're pulling together an affair in a matter of days rather than weeks, it's better to aim for a goal that we have a chance of meeting than to throw a High-Falutin' flop.

It might make your mother cry to hear it, but even a wedding should be Falutin' or Just Falutin' Around if you're holding it at the last minute. In fact, it might be better to reconsider a last-minute wedding—you won't have time to learn that your significant other has a secret yearning to become a trial lawyer and live in Massachusetts, and (maybe more important) you certainly won't have time to register.

A last-minute party is one of the few times that a phone invitation is acceptable. When calling, apologize for phoning at the last minute, and explain why you're doing so. "Aunt Agnes just showed up at our door, and we want to throw a dinner to welcome her," lets the guests know that you didn't overlook them, or you aren't looking to fill out a party with last-minute guests.

A PEARL GIRL KNOWS

If you are running late and don't have much time to invite your guests personally, it is better to enlist the help of a friend or family member than to e-mail. A personal contact, rather than a cold electronic summons, is better even if you aren't doing the calling yourself.

If you are determined to throw a Falutin' party at the last minute, being organized is especially important. Before you start, take the time to sit down and make a detailed to-do list. Order it so that when you go out to run your errands, you do it in an organized way. For example, if the grocery store is a mile from your house, the florist two miles down the way, and the bakery one mile past that, plan to drive to the bakery and then work your way back. If possible, phone in your orders before you leave.

For a last-minute party, you can't beat cheatin'. Buy your invitations, food, and flowers from a grocery store or restaurant (or Costco or Sam's Club). For your take-out food, you won't have the special touch of homemade, so be sure the food is fresh and plentiful. Better yet, dress it up a bit with some homemade touches. A fresh, homemade salad and fruit (and don't forget those brownies from the bakery) will make even take-out kung pao chicken seem like a healthy, special meal.

Bless Your Heart! How to Get Others to Bring the Salad, the Flowers, and the String Quartet

Pearl Girls might be superstars, but they aren't Superwomen. There's no requirement that we work a full-time job, take care of the kids, and throw together a stunning garden party on a moment's notice. Relying on our friends and our family to help is not cheating, and it isn't failing—it's the way things have always been done in the South.

Pearl Girls know how to bat their eyes and smile just so to get things done, and sometimes our smiles help. Hillary Clinton says that it takes a village to raise a child, but, honey, it takes a whole city to throw together a last-minute party. Follow these five simple strategies to get things done:

1. **Beg.** Turn on the charm and ask very, very nicely. You'd be surprised how willing people are to help once you let them know that you're desperate. Think of it as doing your friends a good deed by letting them do a good deed for you.

2. **Borrow.** When it comes to serving dishes, linens, silk floral arrangements, and music, ask friends if you can use what they own for just one evening. Thanks should be given profusely and publicly. During your party, point out that everyone is eating off of Aunt Cora's beautifully pressed linen tablecloth, and watch her beam.

3. **Trade.** (Now you didn't think that I was going to say steal, did you, sugah?) Can you bake, do taxes, set up a computer? Whatever your skill, promise to trade in exchange for help now. Just be sure that you can follow through—Pearl Girls always keep their promises.

4. **Offer advertisement.** Some florists, bakers, caterers, or photographers will work with you if there's something in it for them. If you are inviting over the entire Women's Club, let it be known as you try to finagle a last-minute reservation. Of course, this tactic

won't work if you're just inviting over Cousin Cletus and the clan, but there are situations when a good word goes farther than a checkbook.

5. **Make giving help part of the fun.** Asking guests to bake their famous jam cake or whip up some of their famous deviled ham would ordinarily be rude at a party, but host a potluck, and your guests will be more than happy to bring the food. Or have a sing-along (yes, some folks still do this, and more should), and your guests will be more proud to bring over their instruments to accompany the music. If helping with the party is just part of the fun, guests will be more than happy to help you. Be creative with your theme, and you'll get all the assistance that you need.

Your Cheatin' Party Heart Won't Tell on You

Throwing together a party in a few minutes doesn't have to mean pizza and beer (though there's nothing wrong with that—most of the men prefer a slice of pepperoni to a crème brûlée anyway).

Bucket o' Beer Party: Run to the store and buy several bags of ice, salsa, chips, and some dips. Drag out a galvanized tub, a cooler, or any other large, waterproof container. Fill with ice. Have each of your friends bring a six-pack or several bottles of their favorite beer. You might want to buy a few unusual bottles of your own just in case everyone brings Miller Lite. Mix up the beers together and get tasting!

The Clan Gets Together

When my family gets together, everyone is part of the fun. We cook up hamburgers and hot dogs with all the fixin's, and we never forget the Varsity Chili recipe a friend gave my mother years ago. I mix up some of my famous potato salad, mixing my potatoes and eggs in a bowl the size of a washtub. . . . It is so gooood! With all the goodies, there has to be homemade ice cream. (We have to be sure to remind Mother to make it ahead of time or she forgets to let it cool in the fridge.)

Sister Rita from North Carolina and I bring tables, chairs, and loads of other things to Brother John's the night before. Brother cleans the downstairs of his house. (Thank goodness there's an excuse, or he'd never do it.) Sister Linda follows orders to carry this and that, and cut up this, that, and the other.

The morning of the party, spouses get stuck on the hot grill (with Linda relieving them every once in a while).

The masses come at 1 p.m. on Sunday, and the fun begins. We catch up on the whereabouts of this one and that one, and see that the kids have really grown. A couple of cousins have professional jobs, but one or two we aren't so sure about . . . like the one who takes her son Dumpster-diving at the Kmart, and I mean that literally.

In the afternoon, all have been fed and taken part in the fun. . . . We relive childhood memories with the cousins. We never really grow up, just add a few pounds and lose some hair.

And a few months from now, we'll do it all again, with a little help from the family.

—Ann Burke
   Huntsville, Alabama

Man-a-Pause Party: When a single girlfriend (or just a girl-friend who wishes she were single for one night) has a crisis, throw her a last-minute man-a-pause party. Mix up some cocktails, bake a batch of brownies (or anything else you don't want to be caught scarfing in front of the boys), and call your girlfriends. Talk about man-aging, man-icures, and man-ners . . . anything but the man in your lives. Take a break and be together, and forget the men for one evening.

Swap Meet: Have guests bring a couple dozen of their fa-vorite cookies. You supply some hot cocoa or cider (a gallon of cider and a couple of cinnamon sticks in a Crock-Pot make an easy, but memorable drink). Even though everyone has baked only one batch, they'll go home with a plateful of different Christmas treats. For a post-Christmas party, have everyone bring their most obnoxious, ill-fitting, or just plain tacky Christmas gift. Have a "regifting" party where everyone gets a laugh. (But for Heaven's sake, don't regift something that one of the party guests gave you!)

Stock-the-Freezer Shower: Ask each guest to bring a casse-role to stock the freezer of a new mother-to-be. She'll be grateful in the coming months when she's too busy or just plain tired to cook, and you just need to supply freezer space for a couple of hours. To keep with the theme, serve some frozen appetizers (heated up in the oven, of course!) and a frozen ice cream cake. With just a couple of minutes at the grocery store, you have an easy party that the new mother will appreciate when she's up to her eyeballs (and nostrils!) in diapers.

My friend, Ms. Dianne, *always makes brownies from scratch. After seeing people ooh and aah over hers, I decided it was time to do a little experimenting. I figure I can keep my lawn presentable or slave in a hot kitchen—there isn't enough time for both. They'd be perfect for any cookie swap.*

Deborah's Super Secret (Don't Tell Dianne) Shortcut Brownies

> 1 box your favorite brownie mix
> 1 large tub cream cheese (not the low-fat kind!)
> 1 bag chocolate chips
> 1 egg
> 1 cup sugar (taste as you mix)
> Paper cupcake thingies

Mix up the brownies according to package directions. In another bowl, mix cream cheese, half the chocolate chips, the egg, and the sugar to taste. Place paper doohickeys (a term we Southerners use to describe anything we don't know the proper name for—and if you're making this you don't have the time to look up proper names!) in a muffin tin. Fill halfway with brownie mix, add a dollop (about a tablespoon) of the cream cheese mixture, and top with more brownie mix. Sprinkle with chocolate chips. Bake (get the correct temperature from the brownie box) until done.

Be sure to hide all traces of evidence that you've cheated. Put the box in a dark plastic bag and hide it outside in the garbage can!

Black and Decker or Victoria's Secret Shower: Get couples together for a new-style wedding shower. Forget decorating delicate petits fours—just fire up the grill (or better yet, get the men to do it) and buy a couple of six-packs. Guests can stock the garage (or a more risqué room), and you'll all have a lot of fun.

Wine Tasting: The wine tasting is the ultimate "cheatin' " party. Not only is it easy to throw together at the last minute, it makes you and your friends feel like gourmets. Choose several bottles—try to stick to one country or region, such as Burgundy, Napa Valley, or even Tennessee—and have the staff at the wine store help you if you don't think that you can easily do this yourself. A variety of decent wines are available at less than ten dollars a bottle. If you live near a Southern winery, such as Château Élan in North Georgia or Breaux Vineyards in Virginia, you might even be able to have an all-Southern wine tasting. Offer a few cheeses, fruits, crackers, and breads to round off the evening, and you have a party in minutes! Put on some classical music (or good old country—just because you love wine doesn't mean you have to be stiff and proper) and enjoy.

Games Night: Like me, you have a closetful of board games and cards gathering dust while the kids play with their computers. So let's put them to use. Supply some snacks and drinks from the grocery store (an hour trip maximum and no long stay in the kitchen for you), and have a night everyone will remember. Adults can play bridge or poker, teenagers can play Risk or hearts (they may talk about how lame it is, but watch them play for hours), and the little children can play Clue or Life. Place wagers with jelly beans or sticks of gum. If your cousin and all his children and grandchildren roll into town, this quick party can keep everyone from arguing about who inherited Grandma's jewelry for a few hours.

Potluck: What other party lets you invite your friends, but requires them to bring their own dinner? Have a theme dinner celebrating a region or culture. Better yet, have everyone bring a dish that celebrates their own heritage, and ask each guest to bring something—a story, a poem, an interesting fact—about their background. You may end up tasting everything from authentic Mexican tamales to Chicken Paprikash. Make sure that you give each guest a category of food (green salad, appetizer, starchy side, dessert), so that you won't end up with too much of a good thing. You supply serving dishes, beverages, and the best music your stereo can provide.

Mullet Mania: A mullet isn't just a fish—it's also a hairstyle favored by your unemployed cousin and the boys down at the junkyard. Long in the back and short on the top and sides, a mullet's business on the top, and a party in the back. And for you, a mullet party is a way to get some serious business out of the way—cleaning out the garage—while partying. Do you have a closet full of size 4 dresses when you're sporting a 12? Do you have a StairMaster gathering cobwebs in your garage? Drag out everything that you need to sell, and have your friends bring over their own basement treasures. Wear your best flannels, torn T-shirts, and big hair. You and your friends can compete to see who sells the most (or the least), and who has the most authentic mullet hair and clothing. Everyone can bring over their favorite trailer-park cuisine (consult the bible of lowbrow cuisine, *White Trash Cooking* by Ernest Matthew Mickler, if you get stuck for ideas). If you don't even remember where your kitchen is, just pop open a can of bean dip and a case of beer.

Five Simple Parties You Can (Almost) Buy at the Supermarket

If you don't have the time to toil in the kitchen for hours (or you just don't want to clog up those little pores in a hot, greasy kitchen), you can still entertain friends. Each of these meals requires nothing more than a trip to the supermarket and a couple of minutes—and I mean minutes—in the kitchen. And each offers a special bit of Southern flavor.

Breakfast

Remember when Mama got up before dawn to roll out those delicious biscuits, fry up some sausage, and make her own pan gravy? Well, I don't know about you, but I need my beauty sleep. An easy breakfast doesn't have to mean a box of doughnuts. Add a bag of lettuce and some salad dressing, and this same meal becomes a hearty brunch.

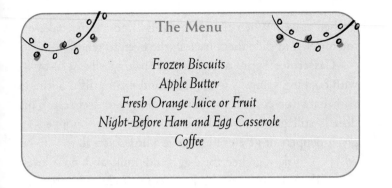

The Menu

Frozen Biscuits
Apple Butter
Fresh Orange Juice or Fruit
Night-Before Ham and Egg Casserole
Coffee

The Shopping List

Coffee
Frozen biscuits
Cooking spray
8 slices bread
½ pound ham (available already cut into cubes if you
    don't know where your knives are anymore) or 1
    package of sausage
8 ounces of your favorite cheese
6 eggs
3 cups milk
Fresh juice or fruit
Apple butter

Directions

Coffee: Make, drink, and get to working!
Biscuits: Follow package directions. When they are
done, leave them on a cookie sheet and cover with a clean

kitchen towel. When the casserole is almost done, take off the towel, and slide them back in the oven to reheat.

Casserole: Spray a rectangular baking dish (12-by-8) with cooking spray. Tear up bread and put in dish. Sprinkle with ham (or crumbled, cooked sausage) and cheese. This dish is still good if you leave out the ham. (Chopped-up green peppers or green onions give a little extra flavor, if you wish.) Whisk together the eggs and milk and pour over. Cover the casserole with plastic wrap or foil, and refrigerate it overnight. Take it out of the fridge while you bake the biscuits. Reduce the oven temperature to 350 degrees F.

Remove the cover, and bake for 35 to 40 minutes or until set. Serve this meal with hot sauce for those of us who want a little fire in the morning. Serve everything with plenty of apple butter for the biscuits and juice to wash it down.

Luncheon

In the North, the Reuben, a gloppy mixture of corned beef, sauerkraut, cheese, and Thousand Island dressing, is the king of sandwiches. The Rayleen is a lighter and more zesty alternative with a bit of Southern flair.

The Menu

Cranberry Spritzers
The Rayleen
Mixed Fruit

Shopping List

Cranberry juice cocktail
Seltzer
Rye bread
Sliced deli turkey or chicken
Deli coleslaw
Sliced deli Swiss cheese
Mixed fruit (precut at the grocery)

Directions

Spritzers: Fill glasses with ice. Pour in a mixture of half juice and half seltzer.

For the Rayleens: Lay slices of bread on a cookie sheet. Top each slice with a couple of slices of turkey or chicken, spread a good dollop of coleslaw on each slice, and top with a slice of Swiss. Run the sandwiches under the broiler until the cheese melts. Place 1 or 2 slices per person on a plate, or put all the slices on a large platter. Serve with mixed fruit.

A PEARL GIRL KNOWS

I've found that the best timer when cooking is the smoke alarm!

Sunday supper meant a spread so that the whole family, and sometimes the preacher, could feast. Ham, slow-cooked greens, sliced tomatoes swimming in that good juice, and fresh biscuits to sop everything up. Best of all, everyone sitting around the table together, sharing stories and resting from a week of hard work. This supper will still let the family get together, but it will let you have some time to put your feet up.

The Menu

Cheatin' Pot Pie
Salad
Shortcut Shortcake

Shopping List

1 store-bought roasted chicken
1 cup frozen peas
1 can of cream of chicken or cream of mushroom soup
¾ cup plus ½ cup milk
7-ounce package of corn bread mix ("just add water or milk" variety)
1 bag of salad greens
Bottled dressing
Ready-made pound cake
Fresh berries
Frozen whipped topping

Directions

Cheatin' Pot Pie: Heat the oven to 400 degrees F. Tear 2 cups of meat and skin off the chicken (you'll have enough left for salads or a couple of sandwiches) and put them in an iron skillet. Sprinkle the peas over the meat. (Don't bother to defrost the peas.) Pour the soup and ½ cup milk over meat and peas, and stir together. In a bowl, mix the corn bread mix and ¾ cup milk. Pour the batter over the chicken mixture. Cook 20 to 30 minutes or until the cornbread is browned and set.

Salad: Mix it up while the Cheatin' Pot Pie is in the oven. Feel free to add chopped fresh vegetables from the greens or the salad bar section of your supermarket.

Shortcut Shortcake: Slice the pound cake, and heap it up with the berries and whipped topping.

A PEARL GIRL KNOWS

My grandma Emma was the most sweet, loving woman I have ever known, and she could make the best dumplings I've ever tasted. She didn't leave me her secret, so I'll give you the only directions that I have: Drive to your nearest Cracker Barrel— and tell them Ms. Grits sent you!

These days, it seems like more and more people don't eat meat. There was a time when Southern food was largely vegetarian of necessity. (Who could afford pork every night?) Since the food was so delicious, no one seemed to mind much. Serve this as a lunch or dinner for your vegetarian guests, and if you want to, heat up a ham steak in a pan for the meat-eaters in the crowd.

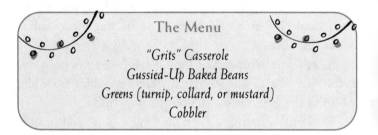

The Menu

"Grits" Casserole
Gussied-Up Baked Beans
Greens (turnip, collard, or mustard)
Cobbler

Shopping List

1 tube ready-made polenta (about 17 ounces)
8 ounces grated cheese (cheddar, mozzarella, Swiss—
   whatever strikes your fancy)
2 cans baked beans (veggie—your guests don't want to
   bite into a big hunk of pork fat!)
Worcestershire sauce, dried mustard, and ground black
   pepper
1 package frozen greens
3 cups fresh or frozen fruit
Sugar
1 tablespoon cornstarch
1 small can of biscuits
Cinnamon
Ice cream or whipped topping

Directions

Grits Casserole and Beans: Heat the oven to 350 degrees F. Slice the polenta into circles, and lay them in a greased 8-by-8-inch pan. Sprinkle the polenta with the cheese. In another pan, mix the beans, a couple of teaspoons of Worcestershire, a teaspoon of dried mustard, and plenty of black pepper. Bake both pans until hot and cheese is melted.

Greens: Follow the package directions. Serve with plenty of hot sauce!

Cobbler: Microwave the fruit with about a ½ cup of sugar until hot. Stir in the cornstarch. Top with the biscuits. (If

---

The Cheater's Best Friend—
Salad Dressing

You may not know a stock pot from a sauté pan, but you can seem like a culinary star with almost no effort. Salad dressing is one of those things that any fool can mix up, but that few people do. Make your own dressing, and the praise you receive will be all out of proportion to your effort. Pull open a bag of lettuce, add some cheese, some chopped vegetables, and some meat (bacon comes precooked these days), and you have a meal on a plate.

Basic Vinaigrette: ¾ cup oil (olive is best), ¼ cup vinegar (balsamic is a good choice), 1 tablespoon Dijon mustard, salt and pepper. Shake everything together in an empty, clean jar.

Additions: Honey (substitute cider vinegar and add a little more mustard), garlic, fresh herbs.

you separate them into layers and lay decoratively across fruit, it is even better.) Sprinkle with sugar and cinnamon. Bake for about a half hour in a 350 degree F. oven while you eat dinner. Serve with ice cream or whipped topping.

Low-Carb Feast

More and more people these days are eating low-carb. Personally, I shudder to think of a world without biscuits, corn bread, and, best of all, dessert, but sometimes your guests will think differently. There's no need to slave in the kitchen over a roast and whipped cauliflower, or, worse yet, ruin God's perfectly good food with fake sweetener, fake bread, and fake pasta. (What is in that stuff, anyway?) This meal will have you out with your guests (and maybe even sneaking a little chocolate truffle while they watch).

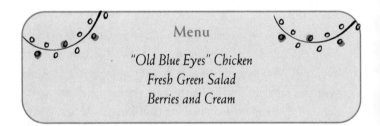

Menu

"Old Blue Eyes" Chicken
Fresh Green Salad
Berries and Cream

Shopping List

Chicken breasts
Bottled Paul Newman Dressing
Salad in a bag
Heavy whipping cream
Strawberries

Directions

Chicken: Heat oven to 350 degrees F. In a baking dish, lay the chicken skin-up, and pour dressing over to cover it. Bake until done, about 40 minutes.

Salad: Toss the salad with some leftover dressing. It's great with extras from the salad bar.

Dessert: While you're eating dinner, chill a bowl and the beater from your mixer in the fridge. After dinner, pour heavy cream in bowl, and whip it with an electric mixer. Pour whipped cream over berries in individual dessert dishes.

A PEARL GIRL KNOWS

For a quick appetizer that almost anyone will enjoy, two words: shrimp cocktail. Get precooked shrimp, and mix up a sauce with mayo, ketchup, prepared horseradish, and lemon juice (in whatever proportions taste good to you).

The Mission Is Never Impossible

It's three o'clock, and your best friend has called you to say that she and five of your girlfriends are coming over in two hours for an evening of fun. Your cupboards are bare, your hair is frizzy, and it looks like your children have dragged the entire Okefenokee Swamp into your living room. You could panic, but that's not the Pearl Girl way. Take the bull by the horns and get moving.

In the nineteenth-century American Southwest, there was a lot of testosterone and nothing much to do but stare at the cattle. Inevitably, this combination produced bulldogging, a form of man-cattle wrestling. If the man had any hope of not being maimed or killed, he had to grab the animal's horns and throw him. From this tactic came the phrase "take the bull by the horns," meaning "to take decisive action."

For an absolute last-second event, the most important thing is to reconcile yourself to the fact that everything will not be perfect. You might be known for your fantastic pastries, but, unfortunately, they take time and energy that you don't have. With an hour or two to go, you better settle for the basics.

1. Choose a decent-looking outfit. If your clothes aren't pressed, hang them by the shower, and set the water on full-blast, or put them in the dryer and set the heat on low.

2. Clean as best you can. Don't be afraid to hide the dirt away in the laundry room or the cupboards. (Why do you think they put doors on those things, anyway?)

3. If you have enough time to run to the store, get some ready-made food. Most grocery stores now carry entrées in the meat department that require nothing more than heating up in your oven. (This is assuming that you aren't hiding your children's dirty soccer uniforms in there.) Serve the entrée along with a cake from the bakery and a store-bought vegetable platter, and you have a hot meal.

4. If you don't have time to run to the store, look up the number of the pizza man.
5. Get alcohol and plenty of it. Enough predinner martinis—sipped, of course—and no one is going to mind the delivery Chinese. If it's Sunday, beg and borrow from the neighbors.
6. Wash your face, comb your hair, and put on your lipstick. You may not have time to look your absolute best, but simple grooming can take you from presentable to stunning.

One-Stop Parties with an Arkansas Native

If you're doing your one-stop party shopping at a Wal-Mart or a Wal-Mart Supercenter, you aren't alone, and you're supporting a Southern company. Sam Walton opened the first Wal-Mart store in Rogers, Arkansas, a little over fifty years ago, and today there are nearly five thousand stores. Southern hospitality is part of the company's success—Sam Walton laid down the "ten-foot rule"—any time you come within ten feet of a customer, greet him and offer help. Honey, that's a good rule whether you're working in customer service or just walking down the street. Wal-Mart is a lot like Southern women . . . all-American but known the world over!

A Lovely Middle-Aged Debutante

We Southern girls can get together anything at the last minute, even a dress (with a little help from Mother). My hometown of Tupelo, Mississippi, doesn't have a debutante ball, but I was invited to the Beaux Arts Ball in Birmingham.

I went abroad the fall of my junior year to Florence. I assumed that by getting home around late December, I would have plenty of time to pick out a dress, get it fitted, shipped and ready to wear for the Beaux Arts Ball in late February. Well, imagine my surprise when my mother called absolutely hysterical, telling me there was no way to get a dress in that short amount of time and I was just going to have to get something in the next two weeks. She gave me two choices: find a dress in Italy or let her pick out a dress for me in the States.

Since I spoke no italiano (how does one say, "I need a deb dress" in Italian?) and I had no idea where to even begin to look for a dress, I opted for the latter. Giving my mom complete fashion freedom was a bit disconcerting, but I really didn't have a choice. We're about the same size, so she went into bridal shops and tried on big white puffy dresses . . . even though she was more than a few years past debutante days. A friend let us borrow a digital camera, so for a solid week, I downloaded pictures of my mom in different dresses, from all angles. Needless, to say, she wasn't smiling in most of them.

The dress ended up working out fine and, in retrospect, my poor mom got the bad end of the deal. She said the girls in the shop thought she was having a mid-life crisis—going into bridal shops, trying on tons of dresses, and making my dad take pictures of her!

—Kirk Reed
   Washington, D.C. (born in Tupelo, Mississippi)

Last-Minute Thoughts for a
Last-Minute Affair

To do a party right, you shouldn't do it at the last minute. Sometimes, unfortunately even we Pearl Girls have to make compromises. Just because we're working at the last minute doesn't mean that we can't use the same charm and creativity that we use for any other kind of entertaining. From an impromptu pizza party after Wednesday prayer group to a quickie wedding (my motherly heart trembles in horror), every gathering deserves the special Pearl Girl touch. You may be dressing up take-out food with your homemade salad, you may be purchasing a few bottles of local wine to liven up a cocktail party, you may be making meals at home in minutes rather than buying them from the store ... whatever you do, you'll add that special little flair to your affair.

Southern Funerals:
The Ultimate Going-Away Party

Where else but the South would a funeral not be complete without a chicken casserole? Funerals in the South have always been not just about grief but also about reminiscing and remembering. In a way, they are homecomings; for the deceased is moving on to his spiritual home and the family and friends are gathering together in their earthly home.

Goodness Gracious!

Drinking liquor and shooting firearms were, until recently, common at funerals in some parts of the South. Unless you plan on having a follow-up funeral, however, I don't recommend bringing back these traditions.

When my father died after a long bout with cancer, I was only ten years old. I remember my aunt Peggy (a nurse) placing quarters over his eyes and pulling a sheet over his head. None of the adults explained these "goings on" to us children. The funeral home took Daddy to be prepared for visitation. They brought the casket back to our living room. Around the clock, friends and family took turns sitting with him—they called it the "sitting up" ceremony. We then drove to the cemetery, the hearse leading the way. There was a sermon on forgiveness, redemption, and a little fire and brimstone. We were devastated, but it does feel good looking back at all the people who took the time to show Daddy respect.

A lot has changed about Southern funerals since my daddy died. Having my aunt cover Daddy, having family and friends sit up to say good-bye, and driving together as a family . . . these old traditions honored him in a special way. Funeral homes and directors have made things a lot easier for families—we don't have to worry about many of the details, and funerals go more smoothly. At the same time, though, family and friends have been taken out of the process, and there was a lot to be said for getting to work at saying good-bye. Still, the important things remain the same. Respect for the family was, and is, the most important part of a Southern funeral.

Then, as now, funerals and wakes featured food, and an abundance of it. Southern funeral casseroles, chicken and dumplings, buttermilk corn bread, every kind of bean possible, sliced tomatoes, relish, mashed potatoes, fried okra, ham, fried chicken, sweet iced tea, barbecue, all kinds of pies, cakes, pudding . . . bringing food is the Southern way of saying I'm sorry and I don't know what to say, but I'm here for you. Food is nurturing. We may have lost someone we love, but we've got to go on living.

After the funeral, it is customary to visit at the home of the deceased. Family and friends visit for hours, and if they don't ease the pain, at least they share it. Southerners tell stories about the one we've lost—how he used to get in no end of trouble (and how many times he got away with it), how he met and fell in love with his wife, how he never could quite bag a deer, how he loved his children more than anything. We remember, we share, and we even laugh a little. Funerals are, in the end, about the living. They're about sharing, about easing the pain, and about being together as a family.

CHAPTER 7

Showtime!
The Day of the Party

The summer picnic gave ladies a chance to show off their baking hands. On the barbecue pit, chickens and spareribs sputtered in their own fat and a sauce whose recipe was guarded in the family like a scandalous affair.

—MAYA ANGELOU
ST. LOUIS, MISSOURI

It is equally wrong to speed a guest who does not want to go, and to keep one back who is eager. You ought to make welcome the present guests, and send forth the one who wishes to go.

—HOMER
THE ODYSSEY (SOME THINGS ABOUT ENTERTAINING HAVEN'T CHANGED.)

*Y*OU'VE CLEANED YOUR HOUSE FROM TOP TO BOTTOM, ironed the tablecloth, arranged the flowers . . . You've worked hard for this day, and it's finally come. If you've planned right, you just might be able to spend the morning doing your makeup or relaxing with your feet up. More likely, though, you'll be running all over town for last-minute details and trying to remember where you left the candles. Just remember: It's all about having fun. If the flowers are a little droopy or the potatoes are a little burnt, it doesn't really matter. Like life, no party is ever perfect, and those little problems are just part of the fun.

Fixing Preparty Amnesia

Your house is immaculate, turkey is roasting in the oven, the flowers are arranged just so, your nails are polished . . . and then, goodness gracious, you remember. Maybe it's the cake for a birthday party, maybe it's the marinade for the meat, maybe it's the present for the guest of honor. You're bound to wake up on the morning of the party and remember what you should have remembered days ago. All hostesses get preparty amnesia about something, but a Pearl Girl hostess knows how to keep her wits and get things fixed.

1. Take a deep breath and keep yourself calm. You won't fix the problem by panicking.

2. If it's something that can be bought, do it. Don't try to bake a cake, arrange flowers, or knit some baby booties on the day of the party. Store-bought dessert may lack your special touch, but you won't mess up your kitchen, your hands, or your timing.

3. If someone else can attend to the problem, put him on the case. Just be careful, though, to give detailed and specific instructions. If you send your husband for cheese and crackers, he may come pack with Cheez Whiz and saltines. There's nothing wrong with Cheez Whiz and saltines, mind you, but they don't really belong at a fancy wine-and-cheese party. Be detailed in what you ask for, and, better yet, write down exactly what you need.

4. Can you do without it? Some things are really necessary, like a main dish at a dinner party or a cake at a birthday bash. Some things are not—the salad course, an extra side dish, or another CD for your collection. Remember, even if you've had your heart set on something special, your guests probably won't even miss it.

5. Can you replace it? If you forgot to put on the roast, and there's just an hour left, it may be time to substitute more quick-cooking fish or shrimp. If you were planning floating tea lights on the table, can you substitute tapers instead? You may not have the party you envisioned, but you can still have a good time. Just keep that positive Pearl Girl attitude, and make do with what you have.

6. Know when to apologize and when to keep your mouth shut. If you kept the guest of honor waiting for hours at the airport, by all means give your most heartfelt, fawning apology (and repeat as necessary). If your guests wouldn't know the difference, though, it's better to keep quiet. They may be eating ham from the grocery store rather than your homemade stuffed quail, but they won't miss it if you don't tell them.

Laying Down the Law

The man in your life means well, but, bless his heart, he's a man. He may truly not understand that some people don't think that watching timber sports while burping the alphabet is the pinnacle of entertainment. It's your job to let him know—no cigars, no wacky party shirts (isn't it time the human skeleton T-shirt got "lost" in the laundry anyway?), and no making fun of the guests.

You've worked hard for this day, and there's no reason that muddy work boots at the table, rowdy music on the stereo, or beer-chugging contests should ruin it. It's time to lay down the law. No matter how much he protests, he'll appreciate it in the end.

And while you're at it, you might want to remind him of basic rules of etiquette. He doesn't want to offend by forgetting to hold a lady's chair, but his mind is too busy trying to figure out how to sneak upstairs to catch the baseball scores. Nobody likes to be lectured, so keep it lighthearted, and make sure you cap off any advice with a kiss. Always serve up a little bit of sugar with your sass!

Be sure that you speak to your husband before guests arrive. During the party, it's better to let your husband be himself than to lecture him in front of others. Besides, you can always get that stain off the rug tomorrow.

Set the Mood

Remember the first time that you sat down in a real theater? Your mother ironed and starched your best dress so much that you crinkled when you walked, your patent leather shoes gleamed so that you could see your face in them, and you held your own tiny purse. (Maybe it had nothing but a dime in it, but you felt like a little lady.) You drove downtown, or even to the big city, and saw bustle like you'd never see back home. You sat down in a deep, red velvet seat. Finally, the lights went down and the curtain went up. You held your breath and waited for the show.

A PEARL GIRL KNOWS

For any large gathering, set the thermostat down, way down, well before anyone arrives. You may be chilly at first, but you'll be grateful when your living room is packed full of warm bodies.

Every party, from a High-Falutin' evening ball to a Just Falutin' Around pool party, is like theater. You've got to set the mood. And the first part of that mood is you. As hostess, you've got to be calm, cool, and having fun, so in the weeks before the party, it is a good idea to create a list of what you need to do at the last minute—chill the wine, set out the flowers, turn down the thermostat, turn on the oven, hide your husband's "Billy Beer" collection. That way, when you're rushing around looking for the lighter, you won't forget to set out the candy dishes or hose down the children. A couple of hours before the party, bring out the list (unless you've lost it in the confusion), and consult it.

If you are playing your own music, start it at least an hour before the guests arrive. The hostess needs to have her party face on, and nothing gets you in the mood quite like music. If you're throwing an elegant High-Falutin' affair, the strings of a Mozart sonata will make you feel like the lady that you are. If you're having a Falutin' party, some smooth bossa nova or jazz will get you in the groove. And for that down-and-dirty Just Falutin' Around bash, go ahead and throw on some Shania Twain (or good old rock 'n' roll). Of course, if you're throwing a High-Falutin' event with live music, you won't be able to have that string quartet start early (at least if budget is any consideration). Even so, go ahead and listen to something elegant in the car or the kitchen. It will put you in the mood and help soothe those jangled nerves.

When you turn on the stereo, it's time to begin turning down the lights. Bright lights keep the party spirits high, but they also may make guests look older and less attractive. For a Just Falutin' Around party, keeping the lights high (but not so high that every wrinkle shows) also keeps the mood upbeat. For a more elegant High-Falutin' or Just Falutin' Around party, low lights set an elegant and more romantic mood (and make us all look just a little bit better). Soft pink bulbs and candlelight show off the inner prom queen in every Southern lady. If you are hosting a High-Falutin' party at a location other than your home, setting the lighting is one of the reasons that you need to show up long before your guests do. Most managers will be willing to work with you to get the mood just right.

A PEARL GIRL KNOWS

Candles are to adults what campfires are to kids—there's a magical ambience to candlelight that makes any party special.

Remember to have the lights right in every room your guests may enter (and we all know that's just about every room in your home). If you want to keep guests out of a room, it's best to lock doors, turn off lights, and do whatever you can to make the room look uninviting (including stocking it with a sullen teenager, if possible).

You will have set out your candles long before the party starts. About thirty minutes before the party, light them. A long-handled grill lighter works better than a cigarette lighter (which might burn those pretty little fingers once it heats up) or matches (which are dirty and never seem to last long enough).

A PEARL GIRL KNOWS

When planning the party layout, keep your disabled guest in mind—leave wide paths open to maneuver, and don't plan to move up and down the stairs during the party. The most important thing, though, is to treat the guest like anyone else.

Have a room (or at least a corner) set aside for coats and bags. And as the guests enter (after greeting them with a warm smile or peck on the cheek, of course), offer to show them where they can stow their gear. Male hosts should offer to take the coats from their female guests, but if you're a woman, you don't need to help unless your guest is older, disabled, or carrying a big load of packages (gifts for you, I hope!).

If someone shows up early (most likely your sister hoping to catch you with your pants down—literally), offer a drink and then get back to your preparation. Don't feel that you need to drop everything just because your guests are early birds; guests who show up on time shouldn't have to suffer just because some people caught you by surprise. If that early arrival is a close friend or family member, you can set them to work. Let someone else light the candles or open up the wine—your hair is important business that needs tending to.

Ringing the Dinner Bell

We've all been at a dinner party where our stomachs start rumbling but the hostess is too busy gossiping with her neighbors or sipping one too many predinner cocktails to notice. As Pearl Girls, we know to tend to our guests properly.

For any party that does not involve a meal, all a hostess has to do is make sure that the food and beverages are plentiful. You may be serving nothing more than chips, dips, and sodas, or you may have an elaborate cocktail buffet and open bar. Whatever you serve, though, make sure that the bowls and platters are always well supplied. (A good rule of thumb is to remember your halves—nothing should be more than half empty until the party is half over.)

We all know someone who claims to be turning thirty-nine for the tenth time, but a party is not the place to point that out. The custom of serving the eldest woman first works only when there's clearly an eldest woman—Great-grandma is aware that she's a bit long in the tooth. For a gathering of people who are close in age, it's better to serve your guests in order of their seats, or, if you are ushering them through a buffet, to pick them at random.

If you're serving a meal, no one will expect to dive into the food the minute they walk in the door. For a brunch or lunch, expect to serve the food fifteen minutes to half an hour after the start of the party. For dinner (or any meal at which cocktails are served), expect half an hour to forty-five minutes. If stragglers have not arrived, and that waiting period has come and gone, go ahead and start without them. If it's a seated meal and they miss the first course, let them start eating the main course, with everyone else. If they miss the main course, as well, it's polite to fix a plate for them and keep it waiting in the kitchen. Barring an accident or medical emergency (and I mean something more serious than a broken fingernail), no Pearl Girl would ever be so late as to walk in after the main course is served.

If you're serving at the table, it's easy to keep the cool stuff cool and the hot stuff hot, but buffets are a bit more difficult. Place out items that aren't going to go bad—bread and crackers—before the party. Fifteen minutes before you expect to serve, put the food on the table. Make sure that you have plenty of Sterno and ice out, as well, and not just because the food is more appetizing at the right temperature. Food poisoning doesn't make a very nice party favor!

No Pearl Girl likes to be the first person to jump into a buffet line. Even if her stomach is threatening to revolt and seize the shrimp cocktail on its own, a Pearl Girl will stand by and wait for others. As the hostess, it's your job to get people started eating. Usher your guests to the buffet in small groups (starting with the guest of honor or the eldest woman). If you still have trouble getting them started, take an empty plate and hand it to someone.

Buffets without Botulism

1. *Don't return cooked meat, chicken, or fish to the dish that held raw food.*
2. *Throw out any marinade that has touched raw meat.*
3. *Keep all meat, chicken, fish, and mayonnaise-based dishes chilled in the refrigerator or packed on ice. On the buffet table, periodically check that there's sufficient ice.*
4. *Keep all utensils clean.*
5. *Don't let leftovers sit for more than an hour without refrigeration.*
6. *Keep hot stuff hot. Make sure that all burners on chafing dishes are functioning, and replace the Sterno promptly when the cans are empty.*
7. *Little hands often have big germs. Offer to fix a plate for any of your young guests, or gently hint that the parents should do it. "Cousin Erma, would you like to fix a plate for little Jim Bob before everyone else goes through?"*

A Turkey of a Thanksgiving

It was the first Thanksgiving hosting the rest of the family. The gathering would include my father and three brothers. I wanted my father to be proud of his daughter, my husband to be proud of his wife, and my brothers—Well, I just wanted to make sure they couldn't tease me.

My husband and I had not been in our new apartment long, and we were still surrounded by boxes, but I took the time to carefully unwrap my mother's crystal, my great-grandmothers' china, and my grandmothers' silver serving pieces.

For weeks, I had planned the menu and shopped for the items I needed. Days before, I began baking green bean and squash casseroles. The night before, I made homemade corn bread for everyone's favorite dressing. (Don't call it stuffing in my house!) I baked homemade pecan and apple pies for dessert. Everything was going so smoothly, I thought I could host more family functions.

The next morning, I checked the to-do list, and everything was right on track. I made hors d'oeuvre platters with homemade deviled eggs, celery stuffed with cream cheese, and sausage balls. I couldn't figure out what all the fuss was about—entertaining was easy. I even told everyone that I didn't need any help—this was a piece of cake.

The house smelled wonderful. The table looked gorgeous. I was so proud as I put the turkey in the oven.

The whole group arrived and proudly said that everything looked and smelled great. I was so far ahead that I even took time to watch a little football with the boys. I told them that I had no idea why women complained about how hard it was to entertain.

An hour and a half into the game, my brother disappeared into the kitchen for a drink. A few minutes later, he called in my husband.

One by one, the menfolk disappeared into the kitchen. Figuring that they were snitching food ahead of the meal, I got up to chase them out.

That's when I found the men gathered around the oven. They weren't snitching food—they were trying to prevent salmonella. They were trying to get the turkey done without my knowing that I had forgotten to turn on the oven. That turkey was as cold and uninviting as a New England winter.

Thanksgiving would have to wait an extra couple of hours that year, and I took the good-natured ribbing in stride. (Pretty is as pretty does, my mother always said.) I learned a valuable entertaining lesson that year. Never strut around like a peacock, or you'll end up looking like a turkey.

—Donna Pope Lawley
Lakeland, Florida

Staying Cool When Things Get Hot

No matter how much you plan, there's a reason to stock up on fire extinguishers, garbage bags, and club soda before a party. Something is bound to go wrong. Part of being a real Southern girl is laughing at yourself when things get hot. Repeat to yourself, "It's only dinner . . . it's only dinner" (or a bridal shower or a wedding). Life's celebrations should be joyful, even when things go wrong.

Food Fumbles: When the roast is dry, the toast is burned, the soufflé is flat, and the aspic looks like tomato soup, the first thing to remember goes against everything that Pearl Girls have been taught—don't apologize, or if you must, apologize once and get it over with. Nothing ruins a meal faster than a hostess telling everyone how terrible everything tastes—again and again and again.

Do what you can to fix the food, but if you can't, the quickest and easiest solution is ordering out. And remember

The Date's No Detail

My childhood friend, Karen Pressnell Duncan, and her partner, Janice Hill Herring, run a lifestyle consulting business, Interior Motives (don't you just love it?!) in Birmingham, Alabama. Details are everything to these ladies, and they never fail. Since these Southern ladies have been raised right, they give their clients more than beautiful homes—every year they welcome their clients into their own homes for a wonderful party.

At a recent party, no details were left to chance. Karen called the caterer at least three times on the day of the party to go over the details.

Thirty minutes before the party, the lights were turned down, the candles were lit, the soft music played in the background . . . but there wasn't a sign of the caterer. Karen had confirmed the delivery time with the caterer—problem was she had forgotten to verify the date. The caterer was sitting back relaxing at home and not a thing was cooked. Realizing the mistake, Karen and Janice fell into action. They sent their husbands out for fruit and cheese trays, and called the caterer to throw together all the food in her fridge for an improvised dinner. Thank goodness they had their own bartender and a well-stocked bar! An hour or (and a few martinis) later, the guests walked into the dining room for a tasty dinner (even if it had everything from the caterer's fridge but the baking soda!).

that a delicious dessert can soothe the wound of wilted lettuce. Have a carton of ice cream on hand—if all else fails, butter pecan heals all wounds.

Candle Crises: Have a fire extinguisher on hand just in case. I once attended a party where a guest leaned too far back and caught his suit jacket on fire. Quick thinking avoided serious burns, but you never know when a toupee is going to topple into the candelabra or a scarf is going to drift into your pillars. If wax drips, immediately place the candle on a safe surface, but don't spend your party trying to clean up spilled wax. The spill is often easier to clean once it has hardened, and anything short of a fire can be mended later.

A PEARL GIRL KNOWS

If I had my life to live over, I'd make the same mistakes, only sooner. —Tallulah Bankhead

House Horrors: If something breaks during the party, forget about it (after picking up the pieces, of course). You'll have plenty of time to worry the next day. The best thing is prevention. Put away fragile and valuable objects before the party starts.

Always have several types of stain lifter on hand, at least one for carpet and furniture and another for clothing. If the stain is on something you own, try not to get upset. Most guests did not intend to spill. (And if they did, you probably shouldn't be inviting them to your parties.) Clean up the

Fixing Food Failures

Oversalting: *In a soup or a stew, add a whole, peeled potato and cook for several minutes. Remove the potato before serving.*

Lumpy Gravy: *Pour the gravy through a fine mesh strainer.*

A Solid Mass of Gravy: *Your thickener has worked a bit too well, or you've made it too early. Slowly stir in some more liquid over the heat until it loosens up.*

Skin on Puddings and Sauces: *To fight in the first place, lay plastic wrap directly on the food and remove just before serving. After the fact, just peel off the skin, stir to hide the residue, and serve. No one will know.*

Dry or Tough Meat: *Instead of serving the meat whole, slice it into thin pieces (to counteract the chewiness). If you have a sauce or gravy, pour it over the top. If not, heat a bit of broth and pour it over the meat.*

Burnt Food: *If one element of your food burns (the onions for the soup, the mushroom topping for the meat), throw it out rather than having the whole dish taste burnt. If the exterior alone is burnt (the peel of a pepper or the outer layer of meat), cut it off and serve only the inside. If the whole thing is burnt, throw it out. There's no hope once the food is incinerated.*

Overspiced Food: *For a creamy curry, add a bit of sour cream. (Stir some hot liquid into the cream before adding, or you'll have a separate food fumble—curdled food.) For a chili or other noncreamy soup, serve with a generous shredding of cheese, a dollop of sour cream or yogurt, and lots of corn bread. Remember, carb-laden foods and dairy will fight the heat, but water and other drinks will only spread it around.*

Fallen Soufflé: *Soufflé? What soufflé? You were making your guests an omelet, right?*

worst, and leave the scrubbing for later. If the stain is on a guest's clothing, offer them the appropriate stain remover, and if it is really big (four-year-old-plus Super Soaker plus red wine) offer them a change of clothing and try to remove the stain.

A Bridal Luncheon to Remember

My niece, Laura, was getting married, and all the ladies had gathered next to the old plantation home, Walnut Grove, to give her a luncheon. The ladies were dressed in their "Sunday-go-to-meeting" clothes, the flowers were in bloom, the birds were chirping, and everyone was content after the fried chicken, potato salad, baked beans, and ice-cold sweet tea.

Everyone was awaiting dessert, an old family recipe—homemade peach ice cream made in an old-fashioned freezer. Suddenly, from out of nowhere came my big, friendly puppy, Frisky. He plowed through a small child's wading pool, splashing water over the ladies standing nearby. Then he splashed in the mud and went from guest to guest, smearing mud on their beautiful dresses as he "greeted" each one. My sister-in-law, Ann, went into action and began to chase the dog. Just as she was about to pounce, she stepped in the mud puddle and went in headfirst. Everyone had to laugh as Frisky licked her face.

We went from disaster to delight as everyone began taking pictures and laughing heartily. It may not have been the bridal luncheon we planned, but everyone enjoyed the party. We still laugh when we look at the pictures of ladies in their mud-splattered best petting the dog. Southern girls always know how to make the best of any situation—just add a laugh and a smile.

—Jean Robinson
Cartersville, Georgia

Dress Disasters: You plan your outfit for weeks and pick the perfect dress to flatter your not-twenty-anymore figure, when your five-foot-ten-inch 120-pound friend shows up wearing the same dress. My goodness, you've been out-blonded—at your own party! If you have time and an extra dress, laugh and compliment her on her exquisite taste; then go up and change. It is better to wear a less-than-ideal dress than to compete with your girlfriend. If you don't have another dress, or you are at a separate venue, don't panic. Try to give her a bit of space by sticking to the other side of the room. Whatever you do, don't worry—she's probably just as embarrassed as you are, and you still look fabulous.

A PEARL GIRL KNOWS

If insects attack a guest, treat a bite with a paste of baking soda and water. If a bee stings, use tobacco paste. And don't forget to tell them that those critters bit them only because they're so sweet!

Visitor Victims

When the dog bites, when the bee stings, when they're feeling bad . . . it is time to tend to your guests. Before a party starts, have a first-aid kit, an ice pack, and the relevant emergency numbers on hand. With any luck, any mishaps will be minor. If something more serious happens, don't panic. Administer first aid if possible; then drive your guest to the hospital (if you haven't been drinking) or call an ambulance. If there's any question at all, err on the side of caution. It's better to look foolish and bring a sprained ankle to the emer-

The Dress

When I was growing up, girls would travel to our house from miles around for my mother's fabulous dresses. With nothing but a picture and some measurements, she could create a dream in taffeta and lace. A girl could go to a fancy boutique for an almost-perfect dress, or she could get one from my mother to fit every curve and flatter her complexion with the perfect fabric. Since Mother was raising us on her own, I didn't dream of coming out with the wealthier girls, but I did dream of wearing those beautiful dresses.

One dress in particular captured my dreams. The cut showed off my figure to perfection, and I looked like a princess above those folds of fabric. I dreamed of dancing in that gorgeous gown, and in those dreams, the most handsome man at the ball would always whisk me away. Unfortunately, Mother made that dress for someone else.

Then from out of the blue, I received an invitation to one of the finest events in Birmingham. Nothing I had in my closet would be good enough to wear, and I couldn't afford to go shopping in some upscale store. I begged my mother to make me a copy of that dress, and she finally gave in and sewed it for me.

The big day arrived. I spent all morning doing my hair, and when I pulled on that dress, I looked like the most beautiful girl in the world. When I entered the room with my escort (almost as handsome as that boy in my dreams), I felt like the belle of the ball.

I felt like the belle of the ball, that is, until I saw it—the dress. My mother's client was standing across the room wearing the exact same dress. Even though I felt like the belle of the ball before I saw her, I could have easily become the belle of the bar—if I had been old enough to drink!

I spent the rest of the evening trying to stay as far away from "the dress" as I could. At the time, it felt like a disaster, but looking back, I can laugh. I also learned a valuable lesson—when it comes to dressing (or life), don't copy anyone else's dreams of perfection. Make your own.

—Deborah Ford
Birmingham, Alabama

gency room than to have a guest with an untreated broken bone.

Rude, Crude, and Socially Unattractive . . . Dealing with Problem Guests

The best way to deal with bad behavior is to stop it before it starts. The hostess sets the tone for the party, and she should do it from the minute that guests walk in the door.

A Tealess Party

Not long ago, I had a party disaster of my own. I hosted a little bridal tea for my friend's daughter, Leslie. Leslie is marrying an Irish gentleman, and several of his friends and family members came along.

Now, I've been to dozens of teas in the South during my life. I've been served everything from lemonade to wine spritzers, but never tea. I served a lovely punch and enough coffee to float away half of Birmingham. Even so, my Irish guests looked puzzled when they saw the table. They said that everything was lovely . . . but where was the tea? They said it again and again, and they had those great Irish accents that made everyone take notice.

I stood over a stove boiling water and wondering whether I was doing it right. (Goodness knows those Irish girls know more about hot tea than I do.) While I made my last-minute tea, I vowed never again to host a tea party without tea, especially if our friends from across the pond are there.

—Deborah Ford
   Birmingham, Alabama

If your guests start to get rowdy, it's your responsibility as the hostess to keep things under control. There's a fine line between having a good time and being out of control, and even Southern ladies and gentlemen sometimes cross it. If things start to get a little wild, turn down loud music and switch it to something soothing. Turn up low lights. Enlist the help of a calm friend to stow away any extra alcohol. If things are still too rowdy, turn the music off and the lights up all the way. And if all else fails, call the police.

Set the Tone

- Greet every guest at the door with a smile. Do not let your cousin stand at the door just to give him something to do, especially if he's had one too many kamikazes. Give each guest attention and make them feel special.
- Make sure you know something about each guest.
- Remain positive throughout the party. Share good humor, and avoid telling embarrassing stories.
- Change the subject if need be (the fate of the local baseball team, the state of the stock market, and even the terrors of local traffic can shift an uncomfortable subject quickly).
- Let your husband eat as much as he wants. Try not to reprimand him in public (bless his heart).
- Don't hesitate to interfere in unpleasant situations, but always do so with a smile—flattering plus firmness will diffuse most situations.
- If a guest needs to be called down, do it quietly and discreetly.
- And remember, never invite an ex-husband (or his family) if you cannot treat him with respect.

If guests quarrel, try to reroute their behavior. Be friendly but firm, and whatever you do, don't take "sides" in the matter. A lighthearted or funny remark works wonders to redirect and diffuse their behavior.

Disaster Doozies

There are party disasters, and then there are party disasters. When something goes horribly, terribly, grievously wrong, try to keep in mind that, if nothing else, you'll have a good story afterwards.

The Dawg:

Dogs are dear, sweet animals, but they have about as much discretion in eating as Elizabeth Taylor on a bad day. If you don't keep an eye on them, they can make off with the turkey, the ham, or—this one was a disaster to end all disasters—an entire pound of fudge, which is poisonous to dogs. At best, you'll lose your party food. At worse, well, let's just say I don't want to be your carpet cleaner.

If your dog has eaten something, first call your vet to determine if it is poisonous. Since you're a Pearl Girl, I'm sure your pet's health comes first, so attend to the animal if need be. If what he's eaten is a danger only to your floors and your menu, send him out into the yard; then take emergency measures inside. Remove as much of the mess as you can with paper towels or rags—the acid in the vomit can wreak havoc on your carpet. Sprinkle the area with baking soda, allow it to dry, and then vacuum. Then apply club soda, blot, and see if the stain is still there. If you still have a stain, use a commercial stain remover or call a rug cleaner. To replace the food, order out, and don't forget to tell your guests the story!

Mother Nature:

Mother nature doesn't like having us Southern girls forget her—so she sends us a little hello every once in a while with tornadoes, hurricanes, and forest fires. If there's a natural disaster threatening your party (or taking off your roof the night before), no one will blame you for canceling. In fact, it's your duty as a hostess to call off the party before you put any of your guests in danger.

We Pearl Girls have been known to smile in the face of danger and party away while the wind blows—hurricane parties are a fixture in coastal communities. While I wouldn't recommend hosting one, if you are a Pearl Girl who never met a tropical storm she didn't like, make the most of a bad situation and face the winds with a smile and a handful of your best and bravest (or most foolhardy) friends.

Bouncing Baby:

Sometimes baby can't wait for his baby shower (and in some families, the wedding) to see his mommy. While I can't blame the little guy or gal from wanting to see his wonderful Pearl Girl mother, it makes it hard to hold the shower if Mommy is off at the hospital, so you'll have to delay. If baby is born and healthy, go ahead and host the shower. If baby's health is in danger, hold off until he gets better, but be sure to let Mommy know you're praying for the little one.

If Mommy is going to be a few pounds lighter walking down the aisle, it's up to her whether she wants to have a public wedding. Some folks think it's tacky to have the baby at the wedding. While I understand this feeling, I think it's good that they're showing their desire to raise the child in a complete family, even if it's a little late. And besides, Mommy will look much better in that dress without baby inside tagging along.

The Chippendale Is Toast:

The thing about antique furniture is, it's old. And as my creaking bones let me know more each year, old stuff tends to crumble and break. (Don't worry, sugah, I'm taking care of myself.) If you put your delicate antique furniture out for your guests, they may very well be daring and actually sit in the chairs, and if they do, those chairs might break.

Strange as it may sound, it isn't large people doing most of the breaking. It may surprise some people, but overweight people know that they're on the heavy side, and they'll avoid delicate furniture. It's your skinny little friends, with all that energy bouncing around inside them, that are more likely to pose a danger to the Louis XV. When this happens, don't joke about them putting on the pounds, no matter how thin. Even skinny little women often have issues with their bodies, and you don't want to add to their embarrassment.

If your heirloom furniture is damaged, take it out of the room and put it away immediately. Don't make your guests feel bad—it was an accident, after all. The next day, take the furniture to an antique specialist. Don't take it to the guy on the corner, and whatever you do, don't fix it yourself. I once had a friend who "fixed" the finish on her antique table, and when she had it appraised the next year, she found that she had turned a ten-thousand-dollar heirloom into a two-hundred-dollar garage sale piece. Those antique specialists can work wonders, so don't despair. And if all is lost, at least you have an excuse to hit the flea markets for a brand-new heirloom.

Alien Abductors:
Once you've determined that it isn't your son in a mask, lay off the hooch. As wonderful as your party is, no one from Mars wants to crash it.

It's Only a Party

No matter what happens the day of, just remember that it's only a party. Even if the quiche jiggles, the cake is flat, and you have a case of the hives, the party can still be fun if you can laugh along with your guests at your problems. Plan ahead, and stop problems before they start, and by all means fix what you can, but also know what can't be fixed. Party punch and favors are all well and good, but it's you your guests really care about. So keep a smile on your face, and everything will be all right.

Deck the Halls, Walls, . . . and Bathroom Stalls, 'Cause Santa's Comin' to Town

> Forget all our cares, drop travail, ignore poverty.
> Eat, drink, and be merry, it's Christmas time.
> Whatever you do, be merry.
> —FERROL SAMS, *THE CHRISTMAS GIFT*

From Gatlinburg, Tennessee, to Branson, Missouri, to St. Augustine, Florida, huge Christmas stores selling everything from traditional strings of lights to your favorite racecar drivers dressed as Santa are packed with visitors . . . in July. Christmas is not just a one-day holiday in the South; it's an event we prepare for all year round (and a few of us—I won't mention names—even keep our Christmas lights up all the way till Easter).

When Thanksgiving rolls around, we drag out boxes of decorations from the basement or attic. More than one Southern lady has an entire room (or rooms) in her house devoted to storing her Christmas decorations. In the typical Southern home, the front yard features reindeer and nativity scenes. The bushes, trees, and house itself have thousands of lights. The front door and windows are festooned with ribbons, lights, and greenery. Inside, ceramic Christmas villages, stockings, and, of course, Christmas trees as high as the ceiling grace every home. (Why, even some of my Jewish friends get into the act with a "Hanukkah Bush"). Maybe we're making up for the fact that throughout most of the South, there's hardly any chance of a white Christmas, but, whatever the reason, it sure does look pretty around here.

And the food . . . Well, I just have one book here, so I can't mention every Christmas goody, but what Southern table doesn't have at least a ham, green bean casserole, oyster dressing, candied sweet potatoes, yeast rolls, sweet potato pie, and a big coconut cake? Not to mention one or two recipes that every family reserves for special holidays.

Ambrosia—a dish made with oranges and coconut—graces many Southern holiday tables. The making of ambrosia is surrounded by the same sort of heated debate that surrounds corn bread. Each family has its own recipe, and each is sure that its version is the only authentic ambrosia. Some add sweetener, some cherries, some bananas, and some (horrors!) marshmallows. However your family makes it, it is delicious, and the Southern table wouldn't be the same without it.

As special as those decorations and those holiday treats are, we Southerners don't forget the true meaning of the holiday. It isn't about the candles or the lights or the cranberries or even the gifts (though I wouldn't mind a new bracelet, sugah). It's about the birth of our Lord and Savior, and loving our fellow man. So, Merry Christmas, whatever the time of year (and don't forget to save a piece of pie for me).

Goodness Gracious!

Dr. Pappas and his wife always decorate their home by wrapping it with a huge red bow. When people ask if it's hard to get that big bow up on the roof, he answers, "It sure is . . . but not nearly as hard as getting the ribbon under the house!"

A Very 'Bama Christmas

You know it's Christmastime around here when the line of cars begins snaking through the neighborhood. No, we don't have a mall or a church or even a Santa Claus around here ... we have Dr. Higginbotham.

Dr. Higginbotham begins preparing for Christmas on January 2—that's right, he takes only one week off. He even has a personalized license plate proclaiming him SANTA C.

His Christmas lights are permanently attached to his house and trees (and for the past couple of years, strung across the street between the telephone poles). He has a working train, a bubble machine, and a child-size village. On some nights, his full-size sleigh is manned with live reindeer. To power the light display, he had to have an extra power box installed on his house. He has so many decorations on his roof and in the trees that he bought an industrial cherry-picker to move him up and down, and it's a good thing, too, since the year before he bought it, my husband rescued him from a twenty-foot fall. If we hadn't spotted him clinging to the gutter, he might not be around to decorate another year.

Not all the neighbors love the Christmas display. One neighbor called the police to report that he was keeping a "dangerous animal" within city limits—it turned out to be a llama. Another year, he had a blimp that said GO 'BAMA on one side and MERRY CHRISTMAS on the other. Someone (an Auburn fan, no doubt), shot it down with a pellet gun—three times. Most of the neighbors, however, are more than happy to play along. In fact, we have one of the best streets in north Alabama.

When Christmas finally rolls around, Dr. Higginbotham dresses as Santa, and his children get into the act as elves and even as the Grinch. People come from all over the city to wander through the yard and gawk at the display.

Of course, being next door has its drawbacks, especially the cigarette butts and half-eaten candy canes that litter my yard every morning. At first, that garbage really annoyed me, but now I have to admit it: Christmas wouldn't be Christmas without Dr. Higginbotham (and a live reindeer or two).

—Lesley Witter
  Huntsville, Alabama

CHAPTER 8

Bring Down the Curtain

*If all the year were playing holidays, to sport
would be as tedious as to work.*
—WILLIAM SHAKESPEARE
HENRY IV, PART I

*Always do sober what you said you'd do drunk.
That will teach you to keep your mouth shut.*
—ERNEST HEMINGWAY

THE CAKE IS CUT, THE LAST COCKTAIL WEENIE EATEN, and your last guest has staggered out the door. It's time to put up your feet, relax, and survey the damage. There are Southern ladies who can't sleep soundly knowing that there are dirty dishes in the house, but I can rest like a lamb. Sure, that dirt is going to be down there to welcome me in the morning, but I think that every good hostess deserves to treat herself to a night of sound sleep. The next morning, you'll have plenty of time to tie up loose ends.

Hello . . . You Must Be Going!

One thing about being a Pearl Girl is that people love us so much, we sometimes can't get rid of them! If you have guests that just don't seem to ever want to leave, keep in mind that it's a compliment to your party-throwing skills.

Generally, Southern ladies stay until their last guest leaves. When you're twenty and partying is your way of life, it's no problem—in fact, you just might suggest a nightcap. Once you reach the age when your joints start creaking around sundown and a night on the La-Z-Boy is more tempting than a night doing the limbo, you'll need some help when it's three in the morning, and you just need to get some sleep. If you cohost a party, or you have a significant other who can serve as host, it's acceptable to say, "I loved seeing all of you, but I need some sleep. I'm leaving my husband in charge."

Five Things a Southern Lady Would Never Do to Get Rid of Stragglers

1. Faking a heart attack, stroke, or food poisoning. (They wouldn't believe you anyway, fabulous cook that you are.)
2. Singing a rousing chorus of "Na na na na, na na na na, hey hey hey, good-bye."
3. Releasing the hounds (or the yippy poodles).
4. Laying down a trail of chocolates (or beer cans) to their cars.
5. Bringing out the big guns—your teenage son's music collection.

As tempting as it might be to introduce those stragglers to the sole of your boot, you'll have fewer regrets in the morning if you use a subtle approach. Start by turning the music down or off and turning up the lights. If guests still don't get the hint, there's nothing wrong with simply saying, "It's getting late, and I think we need a little beauty sleep." Guests would rather you be forthright with them than be embarrassed later about overstaying their welcome.

Sending Them Away Happy
(and Sober if They're Driving)

You don't have to be a Rockefeller (or a game show host) to send every guest away with a parting gift. A little gift by each plate (or in a basket at the end of your buffet table) will make each person feel special. A few weeks before your party, start scouting out the local ninety-nine-cent stores. Little candles, tiny boxes or baskets for candies, and small jars are almost always in stock—just see what they have, and don't be afraid to use your imagination. Give each guest a small chocolate bunny after Easter brunch, tiny bottles of nail polish for a Pearl Girls gathering, a tiny heart with a couple of caramels for a Valentine's Day dinner, or a little piggy bank for your tax-day cocktail party.

Every Pearl Girl takes the time to walk her guests to the door. You don't need to linger with them, but a word of thanks for their time and a quick hug will make every guest leave with a good feeling.

If you have good photographs, it's always a great idea to share them with your guests (because our mamas taught us to share). Send a nice card with the photos to your friends and family. Keep in mind, though, that Aunt Edna may not want to see herself wolfing down her third piece of chocolate cake or slow-dancing with old Mr. McGee. Or maybe she does—even older Pearl Girls like to let loose sometimes.

Since like a true Pearl Girl, you showed your guests a fabulous time, they'll remember your party for years. Just make sure that if they've had too much fun, they take a cab or sleep it off in your guest room. If the party has grown a little wild, it's a good idea to close up the bar before your guests start to leave. Giving them time to sober up (or at least for you to determine whether they've had too much to drive) can keep good memories from becoming tragic ones. It's your party, and your responsibility, honey. (And these days, there are plenty of trial lawyers willing to remind you.)

What's That on the Rug? How to Clean Everything

Most post-party cleanup requires nothing more than a little soap and water. Picking up the garbage, doing the dishes, and scrubbing down the counters are tasks that any Southern girl should be able to do (or better yet, get others to do) without any instructions. After all, those white gloves show every bit of dust, so we like to keep our homes clean every day. A few things are harder to clean, though, so even Pearl Girls need special instructions. If these special cleaning tricks don't work, we can always use the party as an excuse to pursue every Pearl Girls favorite hobby—shopping.

Any Difficult Spill: Rope in husband. Show him the spot. Repeat as necessary.

Wine from Rug: When the spill is fresh, blot (don't rub) to get the excess, then sprinkle salt generously on the spill, and wipe up with cold water. If that doesn't work, use a commer-

A PEARL GIRL KNOWS

All her life my mother told me, "No matter how poor you are, you can always be clean." —Andrew Hudgins

cial rug-cleaning product. If that doesn't work, call a professional rug cleaner. If they can't fix it, you have a perfect spot for a new potted plant.

Cocktail or Juice from Rug: Blot up excess. Apply a solution of 1 part water and 1 part laundry detergent. If that doesn't work, apply a solution of 1 part water and 1 part colorless vinegar. If that doesn't work, call a professional rug cleaner. If that doesn't work, it's time to rearrange the furniture.

Greasy Stains from Cloth: Take up as much as you can with an absorbent paper (paper towels or a brown paper bag). Apply stain pretreatment before washing. If that doesn't work, apply a solution of ½ cup water and 1 tablespoon ammonia to the stain. Let the stain sit, and wash it again. If that doesn't work, go through the process one more time. Do not dry the cloth until the stain is gone, or you'll risk setting it in the fabric. If nothing else works, you just might have some new fabric swatches for quilting.

Mud from Carpets: Gently scrape up as much as possible (being careful not to grind it in). Apply a solution of 1 part water and 1 part laundry detergent. If that doesn't work, apply a solution of 1 part water and 1 part colorless vinegar. If that doesn't work, call in the cavalry. If that doesn't work, it's a good excuse to install that nice new Berber rug.

Spills from Wood Furniture: Clean with a solution of water and wood soap. Clean small sections at a time to avoid soaking the wood. Dry thoroughly with a clean towel. Do not use furniture wax, as it may only produce a buildup over time.

Southern ladies may not gulp down their drinks, but sometimes those little sips sure add up to a big headache the next morning. Even the finest Southern ladies and gentlemen sometimes take a little nip that leads to another little nip that leads to karaoke "Copacabana."

SOUTHERN TRANSLATION

veisalgia [vī sal´ jə] n. *the scientific word for hangover, from the Norwegian kveis, meaning "the bad feeling you have after partying" and the Greek algia, meaning "pain."*

There are about as many recipes for a hangover cure as there are fishing stories, and just like those stories, only a handful are true. If it makes you feel better to down a raw egg, beef broth, and hot sauce the next morning (or pickled herring, or any of the other so-called cures people tout), by all means do so, but you're likely just to get an upset stomach to match that throbbing head and cotton mouth than to cure your hangover.

A PEARL GIRL KNOWS

If you want a less severe hangover, think clear. Drinks high in cogeners (chemicals formed during the processing of liquor) have been shown to cause more severe hangovers. Dark alcohols, such as brandy, whiskey, and dark rum, are higher in cogeners than clear alcohols, such as white rum, vodka, and gin.

If you want a remedy that actually works, the first step is to stay hydrated. Drink water between alcoholic drinks and before you go to bed, and drink plenty more water in the morning. Vitamin B_6 has been shown to lessen hangover effects if taken before drinking, so if you're planning a big night, you may want to take your vitamins beforehand. Honey before drinking may help, as well, as its fructose may help you metabolize the alcohol, and it is rich in vitamin B_6. (Talk about a spoonful of sugar helping the medicine go down!) An over-the-counter painkiller the next morning can lessen your symptoms. While hair-of-the-dog remedies may take away your pain momentarily, you're just delaying the inevitable hangover (and a lady doesn't drink in the morning). Coffee may help the next morning, but if you drink it the night of the party, you won't sober up—you'll just be a wide-awake drunk. In truth, the best way to cure a hangover is not to drink in the first place. Since none of us ever seem to follow this advice (even I've had my share of morning regrets), at least when you're feeling miserable, you'll know you're in good company.

Serving Memories with Class and Sass

Confess. You and I both know that there are shoe boxes full of photos stashed away somewhere in your house. You've been meaning to organize them for years, but somehow you've never gotten around to it, and every year, the jumble grows a little bit higher.

Organizing your pictures won't just clean up that "junk closet" (and make more room for the ThighMaster and the five hundred Beanie Babies)—it'll also help preserve those photos for years to come. Kept in an acid-free album away from heat, cold, and light (and not stashed on top of the old croquet set in a damp garage), your photos will last long enough for your grandkids to laugh at your husband's experiments with sideburns.

Organizing your party pictures is a great excuse to throw yet another get-together. Sit down with your children, your

Making Memories

My mother was about to turn eighty, but she was suffering from dementia and reluctant about having a party. I did not realize how sick she already was, and I really wanted to give her one. So the planning got started. Mom's birthday was in February, and she was concerned we'd have "weather," so we decided to have the party in May. We figured if the Queen could postpone her celebration, we could, too. I made invitations using copies of Mom's baby picture. For the centerpiece of each table, we filled flowerpots with fresh flowers and ribbons, and we topped it off with a little straw hat propped up by a dowel. We strung pearl garlands around each table. We served typical Southern party foods—cucumber sandwiches, strawberries with dip, ham rolls, and iced-tea punch. Instead of one large cake, we decorated little cakes like hats and displayed them on a tiered plant stand. About two hundred friends paid their honors to Mom that day. The memory of all those friends is all the more special because Mom died less than a year later. The months following the party were really difficult, but when times were really hard, we would drag out the pictures of the party and Mom would smile as she looked at all the friends and family that visited her that day.

—Judy Sizemore
Muscle Shoals, Alabama

family, or just a group of friends, and have everyone get into the act. Albums can be purchased cheaply at craft stores, which should also have a scrapbooking section. You can buy the elaborate cutouts and borders that are available to scrapbookers, or you can try a simple approach with nothing but photos and perhaps a few labels. Whatever approach you choose, sorting, labeling, and placing the photos in an album goes a lot faster with the help of a few friends.

If I Do Say So Myself . . . How to Brag on Yourself and Still Be a Lady

Many Southern ladies will never say anything good about themselves. They believe that it is undignified to brag. While I agree that too much chest-thumping will make you look unladylike (or worse yet, like a Yankee), pride is who we are as Southerners.

SOUTHERN TRANSLATION

fishin' [fish´ ən] n. *catching your supper (or losing a lot of crickets and worms) with a rod and reel; the art of getting people to give you the praise you so richly deserve.*

Asking directly for a compliment is no way to get one. You'll never know if the praise is heartfelt, and you might get a reputation as someone who fishes for compliments. A more subtle approach is to brag about yourself, but to give someone else credit for the braggin'. "My husband just loves this cake, so I hope you do, too," or "I can't believe that my mother-in-law had such a good time at the party." While you shouldn't do too much of this, you can get away with drawing out praise while never saying a good word about yourself.

Here in Birmingham, we have a column called "Scribblers," and every hostess aspires to get into it. The same is true of many other Southern towns. Bribing or blackmailing the columnist is no way to get into it. (Though women have tried—believe me.) Sending the social editor a polite notice about your party (and making sure that if she is your guest you know to keep her happy without fawning) is considered fine etiquette, however.

A PEARL GIRL KNOWS

Character is what you are, reputation is what you try to make people think you are. —Anonymous

The best way I know to get praise, however, is to give it. Everyone likes to hear good things about themselves, and I believe that there's something good to say about absolutely everyone. Your next-door neighbor may have the figure of a baby rhino and the disposition of a mangy dog, but if you look hard enough, you'll find those pretty eyes or that gift for sewing. Maybe she'll say something good back to you, or maybe she'll blush and say nothing, but at the worst you'll feel better about yourself for giving someone praise, and at the best you'll exchange compliments till your throat is sore. If no one else praises you, let me start. You're a Southern woman (at least in your heart), you are wonderful, and honey, you can entertain with the best of them.

Come on Back
Anytime, Dah'lin

We Southern girls just hate to say good-bye. It always takes longer than we think—and far longer than our husband would like—to leave a party. We have to thank the host, compliment her dress, and ask one more time for that wonderful pound cake recipe . . . and then she has to tell us how much she likes our new hairstyle. It leaves our poor men shaking their heads and wondering what we manage to talk about for so long. So I just wouldn't be a Southern girl worth her pearls if I let you leave this book without at least one more word!

We Southerners love people, whether they're friends, neighbors, family, or even Northerners (bless their hearts). We have a lot of traditions in the South, and I hope that this book helps preserve a few of them. The most important tradition I know is hospitality—greeting our friends (old, new, and future) with genuine love and welcome. Whatever our religion, we Southern girls know that there's wisdom in this Bible verse: "Be not forgetful to entertain strangers, for thereby some have entertained angels unawares." We Southern girls open our homes and our hearts to everyone, and we're all the richer for it.

I love sharing my feelings about entertaining and our Southern heritage, and maybe I left you with a few laughs (or more likely groans). Whatever the case, if this spurs one woman to dig out her grandmothers' old pickled okra or co-conut cake recipes, I will feel some pride (as long as she sends some on down to me!).

In fact, I think I'll invite some friends over tonight. We Southern girls are too precious to keep locked up in the house—we've got to get on out there and strut our stuff. So put on your party face, put down this book, and let's get entertaining!